Longman Applied Psychology
General editor: Philip Feldman

The social creation of mental illness
Raymond Cochrane

Compulsive gamblers
Mark G. Dickerson

Psychological aspects of pregnancy
Anthony Reading

Forthcoming:
Biofeedback in practice
Douglas Carroll

Chemical control of behaviour
Steven Cooper

Clinical psychology of the elderly
A. D. M. Davies and A. G. Crisp

Drink and drinking problems
Clive Eastman

Behavioural medicine
P. G. Harvey and B. Dodd

Methods of changing behaviour
Andrée Liddell

The schizophrenias
M. J. Birchwood, P. Green and M. C. Preston

Fears and anxieties
D. C. Rowan and C. Eayrs

Institutional care and rehabilitation
Geoffrey Shepherd

The social creation of mental illness

Raymond Cochrane

Longman
London and New York

Longman Group Limited
Longman House, Burnt Mill, Harlow
Essex CM20 2JE, England
Associated companies throughout the world

*Published in the United States of America
by Longman Inc., New York*

First published 1983

British Library Cataloguing in Publication Data
Cochrane, Raymond
  The social creation of mental illness. – (Longman
  applied psychology)
  1. Mental illness
  I. Title
  305'.9'0824   RA790

  ISBN 0-582-29613-7

Library of Congress Cataloging in Publication Data
Cochrane, Raymond.
  The social creation of mental illness.

  (Longman applied psychology)
  Bibliography: p.
  Includes index.
  1. Psychology, Pathological – Etiology – Social
aspects. I. Title. II. Series.
RC455.C567   1983   616.89'071   82-17141
ISBN 0-582-29613-7

Set in 10/11pt Linotron 202 Times
Printed in Hong Kong by
Astros Printing Ltd.

Contents

Editor's preface

In most areas of applied psychology there is no shortage of hardback textbooks many hundreds of pages in length. They give a broad coverage of the total field but rarely in sufficient detail in any one topic area for undergraduates, particularly honours students. This is even more true for trainees and professionals in such areas as clinical psychology.

The Longman Applied Psychology series consists of authoritative short books each concerned with a specific aspect of applied psychology. The brief given to the authors of this series was to describe the current state of knowledge in the area, how that knowledge is applied to the solution of practical problems and what new developments of real-life relevance may be expected in the near future. The twelve books which have been commissioned so far are concerned mainly with clinical psychology, defined very broadly. Topics range from gambling to ageing and from the chemical control of behaviour to social factors in mental illness.

The books go into sufficient depth for the needs of students at all levels and professionals yet remain well within the grasp of the interested general reader. A number of groups will find their educational and professional needs or their personal interests met by this series: professional psychologists and those in training (clinical, educational, occupational, etc.); psychology undergraduates; undergraduate students in other disciplines which include aspects of applied psychology (e.g. social administration, sociology, management and particularly medicine); professionals and trainee professionals in fields outside psychology, but which draw on applications of psychology (doctors of all kinds, particularly psychiatrists and general practitioners, social workers, nurses, particularly psychiatric nurses, counsellors – such as school, vocational and marital, personnel managers).

Finally, members of the general public who have been introduced to a particular topic by the increasing number of well-informed and well-presented newspaper articles and television programmes will be able to follow it up and pursue it in more depth.

Philip Feldman

Acknowledgements

I would like to thank Phil Feldman for his valued comments on various aspects of this work. I am also very grateful for all the help given by Lesley Leigh and Brenda Smith in preparing the manuscript – a task that was made much more pleasant by their willing assistance.

Chapter 1

Introduction

One of the most striking features revealed by the study of mental illness is its variability. Not only is it variable in the way people are affected but the vulnerability of different individuals is also surprisingly different. Someone living in Ireland is more than twice as likely to be admitted to a mental hospital in any one year as someone living in England. A Scot who comes to live in England has a much greater chance of being admitted to a mental hospital than if he or she had remained in Scotland. Women are almost one and a half times as likely to be admitted to a mental hospital as are men. Pakistanis who have come to live in England are one of the least likely groups of all to be admitted to mental hospitals, whereas West Indians are more likely than are the native population to be treated in hospital. Why should these differences exist, and how can they be explained? This is the central question to which this book will address itself. The theme of the answer will be that social factors are largely responsible for the creation of mental health differentials.

Obviously there will be individual and biological differences in the extent to which people are vulnerable to mental illness, but it will be contended that these differences are far outweighed by the impact of the social situation in which people find themselves and, even more importantly, the definition that is placed upon that situation. More than this a person's values and general outlook will influence the extent to which his responses will become defined as indicative of mental illness whatever the underlying psychological state. We have all, perhaps, become more willing to recognize in ourselves and others symptoms of psychological distress than was once the case. In part, at least, this is a healthy but inevitable side-effect of the reduction in the level of prejudice against the mentally ill which has occurred during this century. It does mean, however, that feelings of anxiety or unhappiness which in certain sections of society were once taken for granted as a part of the natural order of things are increasingly being defined as evidence of 'neurosis' or 'depression', with professional help of one sort or another being sought. This is one explanation for the striking fact that in the year 1900 about 90 out of every 100,000 people in the country were admitted to a mental hospital, but by 1977 (the last year for which figures are available) 380 people out of every l00,000 were admitted to mental hospitals. This escalation has undoubtedly been influenced by the increased provision of facilities for inpatient treatment, but this may be nothing more than a reflection of the increasing demand. Even if it were the case that increased availability of beds leads to an increase in demand, this is but another demonstration of the possibility that social forces can create what we recognize as mental illness.

If further evidence is required of the overwhelming importance of social factors in the aetiology of mental illness it can be provided indirectly by an examination of the present state of psychiatry. For most of the major psychological disorders (such as depression and schizophrenia) psychiatry can offer treatment with a good hope of influencing the course of the disorder. However, no one speaks of a 'cure' in relation to these disorders: the most that can be offered to those that suffer from them is some relief from the worst effects of the symptoms. Symptomatic relief is usually effected through physical treatments such as chemotherapy and electro-convulsive therapy (ECT). The basic reason for this unsatisfactory state of affairs is that psychiatry is still committed to treating the individual outside his social context. This, together with the failure to find causes of the disorders within the individual, has led to treatment being developed empirically. The meaning of this is that some drugs have been discovered more or less accidentally to affect radically the symptoms of some psychological disorders. A prime example is the treatment of schizophrenia with neuroleptics which were originally developed to allay medical patients' fears before surgery (Julien 1981: 126).

There is no articulation between theories of the aetiology of many of the mental disorders and theories of treatment. In fact in many cases it is a misnomer to speak of theories underlying current psychiatric treatment practices. It seems that a hope exists that eventually a biological or biochemical basis of the major disorders will be discovered but even if such a discovery should be made it will still only be the uncovering of an intervening variable rather than an ultimate cause. The fluctuations in the incidence of disorders over time, place and social category are too large ever to be explained away by the differential incidence of some purely biochemical imbalance. While this state of affairs persists, physical treatments are bound to be only palliative measures and cannot hope to have any effect on the basic conditions underlying the disorders. It is even less likely that individual psychiatry will have anything to offer in terms of preventing mental illness so long as it persists in intervening at the level of the individual and does not address the person in a social context.

The measurement and meaning of mental illness

It is not intended to offer any systematic, formal definition of the term mental illness. It is assumed that the reader will be familiar with the major categories of pyschological disorder and with the taxonomies most frequently used by psychiatrists and psychologists. However, a word is necessary about the empirical definitions employed by psychiatric epidemiologists whose work forms the basis of many of the arguments to be discussed in this book.

The earliest attempts at plotting the social distributions of psychiatric disorders used as their basic data mental hospital admission rates. This method is in fact still widely used and, by default, mental illness is often considered to be synonymous with admission to a mental hospital. A moment's reflection shows that this is likely to lead to a somewhat distorted view of the total picture. Inpatient treatment is only one of the many forms of psychiatric care that are currently offered and, as we shall see later, many people with psychological disorders never come into contact with a psychiatrist at all. Having said that, it is necessary to recognize that mental hospital admission studies have contributed significantly to the development of psychiatric epidemiology, and in order to properly evaluate their importance it is necessary to know something of their methods.

Studies based on mental hospital admissions typically are interested in assessing the relative incidence of a particular disorder. Incidence is usually defined as the number of new cases of a disorder occurring in a population during a specific period of time (most often one year) divided by the number of people in the population exposed to the risk of the disorder during that same time. This fraction is then multiplied by one hundred thousand so that an incidence rate is recorded 'per one hundred thousand of the population'. It can be seen consequently that the incidence rate is an estimate of risk of developing a disorder during a one-year period. Where incidence rates are to be compared between two or more groups it is usual to standardize them in terms of other variables. Thus, for example, if we wish to compare the incidence rates for depression in black and white people in Britain it would be a good idea to take into account the fact that age is also related to the likelihood of depression developing and that the age structures of the black and white populations in this country differ. A meaningful comparison could only be made on the basis of age standardized rates. It does not stop there, of course, because we also know that the incidence of depression is different for each sex. To get an even more accurate picture, therefore, it would be necessary to sex standardize (as well as to age standardize) the rates of depression in the black and white populations.

Some studies use as their measure of incidence the total number of mental hospital admissions which will include both first admissions and readmissions. Strictly speaking this is not a measure of incidence, although it is often treated as such. It is a measure of the number of occurrences of a disorder in a particular time period which overlooks the likelihood that some people will be admitted and readmitted to hospital for what effectively may be the same episode of illness. In general terms, estimates based upon all admissions do provide a more accurate description of the number of people affected by a disorder during a given period.

This brings us close to the second major measure used in psychiatric epidemiology – namely prevalence. Prevalence is defined as the number of cases of disorder present in the population at a specific time divided by the number of people in the population. Prevalence rate, like incidence rate, is often expressed per 100,000 of the population at risk. One way in which prevalence can be estimated is by a census of mental hospital inpatients on a given day in a particular year. This method is now only very occasionally used in psychiatric epidemiology. Obviously prevalence will be influenced by incidence and by the length of time each patient spends in hospital.

Although the use of mental hospital admission statistics offers some ready advantages to the researcher, particularly their widespread systematic collection by government agencies and their annual publication in a more or less systematic form, their use for research purposes also brings with it some very serious disadvantages. Several of these disadvantages are listed below, while others are discussed in the context of specific studies when these are introduced in subsequent chapters:

1 As has already been stated, inpatient care is only one form of psychiatric treatment. In recent years outpatient and day patient care has been growing more rapidly than inpatient care so that historical comparisons based on inpatient statistics alone will tend to underestimate the increase in psychiatric contacts made in recent times.

2 All hospital statistics are very substantially influenced by the availability of beds. Indeed, in cross-national comparisons of incidence rates probably the major determinant of a country's apparent level of mental illness is the number of mental hospital places available, taken together with the number of psychiatrists available to offer treatment. This obviously tells us far more about the country's economic state and the degree to which it is committed to a mental health system than it does about the incidence of mental illness in that country.

3 For the most part mental hospital admissions limit studies to aggregate data analysis. This means that only very gross generalizations are usually possible. This difficulty becomes even more acute when the independent variable which is being related to men-

tal hospitalization is itself also expressed in the aggregate. A detailed discussion of this problem will be found in Chapter 4 which reports on several studies which have assessed the relationship between the degree of overcrowding found in particular areas of a city and the incidence rates of mental illness in those same parts of the city. It may be imagined how easy it is to fall into certain traps when one wishes to make statements of causality after relating two aggregate level variables.

4 A great many other factors will intervene between the onset of a psychological disorder and admission to mental hospital. There is no reason to think that the intervening variables will be equally or randomly spread throughout the population being studied. Thus differences in the incidence of mental illness as indexed by mental hospital admissions may in fact be measures of some other variable such as willingness to go to a psychiatrist. Some of these potentially misleading variables are discussed in the next section of this chapter.

5 Perhaps most important of all, aggregate level data do not allow the most interesting questions to be asked. Usually very little information is available on each individual who goes to make up an incidence rate. Published statistics on mental hospitalization are not, for example, available broken down by marital status and social class. The absence of any information on such basic demographic variables is bad enough, but information on the more interesting psychological variables is obviously going to be entirely absent from statistics published on incidence levels.

The major alternative to the use of mental hospital admission statistics is the community survey. Originally community surveys were designed to estimate the true prevalence of disorders, as they attempted to uncover the untreated as well as the treated cases of psychological disorder which existed in a particular community at a particular point in time. This was achieved by taking a scientifically drawn sample of the total population and in some way examining each individual in the sample to discover whether or not they should be considered as a case. Other information about the social and personal characteristics of the individuals being interviewed was also usually gathered and on the basis of this information hypotheses about the factors which were important in the aetiology of mental illness were developed and tested.

It soon became apparent, however, that the estimation of 'caseness' based upon community survey interviews was somewhat unreliable. In a survey of forty-four different studies of the rates of psychological disorder estimated by community survey methods, Dohrenwend and Dohrenwend (1969) found rates varying between less than 1 per cent to over 60 per cent. A major cause of this extreme variability was undoubtedly the measure of psychological disorder employed in a particular study. Subsequently the separation of community survey respondents into cases and normals has more or less been abandoned in favour of the somewhat less sophisticated but more reliable approach which treats psychological disorder as a continuous variable. Each respondent in a survey is given a score on a particular measure of psychological disorder which indicates the extent to which they have psychological problems rather than whether they are mentally ill or not.

Although the community survey offers innumerable advantages over the use of mental hospital admissions statistics, it too has some disadvantages. It is not proposed here to go into problems of sampling, response rate and biases introduced by particular survey techniques; however, it is necessary to discuss the exact nature of what is usually measured when such surveys attempt to assess mental illness. Typically, community surveys of psychological disorder rely on a short, standardized inventory to assess the degree of disorder and one such inventory, which is probably the most frequently used in the studies reviewed in this book, is included as Appendix 1. Such scales are typically derived by measuring the kinds of symptoms which frequently appear among those diagnosed as suffering from mental illness and which only rarely appear among those who are considered by psychiatrists to be normal. Obviously, to be useful such a scale must include symptoms which are encountered with some frequency in the general population and cannot therefore be confined to the most extreme and bizarre symptoms of psychotic behaviour. Because of the way in which they have been developed such scales clearly do not give an indication of whether or not a person is mentally ill in the clinical sense so they are not likely to be valid as case identifiers. What they can do is to give a fairly sensitive estimate of the extent to which an individual has psychological traits or 'symptoms' which are characteristic of people who have been diagnosed as mentally ill and which are uncharacteristic of those deemed to be free of mental illness. In other words, the symptoms on the scales occur with a much greater frequency in the mentally ill than in the normal population. However, it is very important to stress that they may not be the defining characteristics of mental illness. In fact this will definitely not be the case for certain psychotic states because the most bizarre and threatening symptoms (such as hallucinations) are not typically included on symptom scales and yet may be vitally important in reaching a clinical diagnosis of schizophrenia, for example. Alcoholism, personality disorders and mental subnormality will also remain undetected by most of these symptom scales.

Such scales are perhaps most usefully regarded as measuring mild and undifferentiated psychopathology, often with a strong psychosomatic component. A person achieving a higher score on such a scale will be in more psychological discomfort than someone achieving a lower score and the degree of discomfort will be roughly proportional to the scores achieved by different people on the same scale. In some cases symptom scales developed for use in community surveys do allow some differentiation between different disorders to be made (for example some specifically measure depression) but it is often found that there is a very high intercorrelation between specific subscales and between subscales and the global indices of undifferentiated psychopathology (Cochrane 1980a).

Many community surveys have confined themselves to estimates of the relative occurrence of psychological symptoms among people who are resident in their own homes at the time of the survey. As this approach will clearly overlook people who are so severely psychologically disturbed as to be confined to a mental hospital (or indeed who are living in any other kind of institutional arrangement or who are homeless), studies of this kind will not give a complete picture. An approach which has been favoured recently is to utilize both data on mental hospital admissions and information based on community surveys in studies of the same phenomena (see, for example, Cochrane and Stopes-Roe 1979, 1981c).

The individual's response to his own psychological state

Many things other than the occurrence of psychological disorder have to happen for an individual to be admitted to a mental hospital. Indeed, many cognitive steps have to be taken before the person himself recognizes or comes to believe that he is psychologically troubled. Figure 1 represents some of the stages involved. What is important here is not solely the fact that many decisions have to be made by people in formulating their own disorder but that these decisions may be made at a differential rate in different social groups.

Goldberg and Huxley (1980) suggest a series of three filters through which potential psychiatric patients have to pass: first, they have to decide to consult a doctor; second, the doctor must recognize that the person has a psychological problem; and, third, he must decide to refer the patient to a psychiatrist who will then take the final decision on whether the person is truly mentally ill or not. Useful as such a model is, it seems hardly adequate to deal with the complexities involved in becoming a psychiatric patient. A more extended model is offered in Fig. 1 which incorporates some of the elements of Goldberg and Huxley's filter model but elaborates further on the cognitive processes occurring in the potential patient.

The example in Fig. 1 concerns the eventual formal recognition of a person suffering from depression but it could equally well be applied to any disorder. It begins with the existence of relatively diffuse psychological and psychosomatic symptoms (such as, for example, early wakening, loss of appetite, lethargy). Even at this stage a number of people will undoubtedly fail to recognize that they have a problem because it may have had an insidious onset or may be attributed to some specifically external cause (such as the weather) or because the problem is masked by other behaviours (such as a gradual increase in drinking).If someone does reach the second stage and acknowledges that a problem exists, there has to be a further decision that this problem is of an emotional or psychological nature. The alternative definition that some people may prefer is that it is due to a physical condition or to some temporary stage in their life, such as the menopause, or because of overwork, and so on. At this stage it is possible to imagine that women may be more prone to recognize their problems as having an emo-

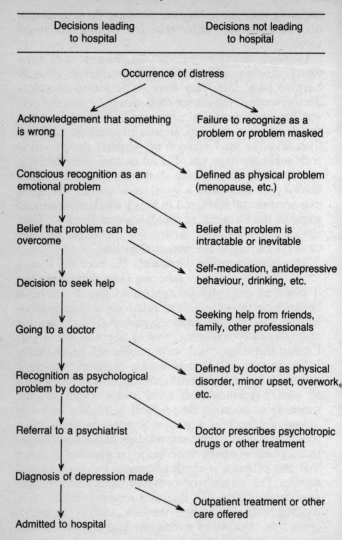

Decisions leading to hospital	Decisions not leading to hospital
Occurrence of distress	
Acknowledgement that something is wrong	Failure to recognize as a problem or problem masked
Conscious recognition as an emotional problem	Defined as physical problem (menopause, etc.)
Belief that problem can be overcome	Belief that problem is intractable or inevitable
Decision to seek help	Self-medication, antidepressive behaviour, drinking, etc.
Going to a doctor	Seeking help from friends, family, other professionals
Recognition as psychological problem by doctor	Defined by doctor as physical disorder, minor upset, overwork, etc.
Referral to a psychiatrist	Doctor prescribes psychotropic drugs or other treatment
Diagnosis of depression made	
Admitted to hospital	Outpatient treatment or other care offered

Fig. 1   Stages in becoming admitted to a mental hospital

tional basis than are men, who may defend themselves against this recognition because it may be considered unmanly to admit to such emotional weaknesses.

A crucial point in the process of recognition of an illness has now been reached. The belief that one is suffering from an emotional problem does not necessarily imply a corresponding belief that this problem can be dealt with or that the situation can be ameliorated. It is here, probably, that one of the biggest changes in the outlook of most people has occurred in recent times. What was once considered an almost inevitable state of affairs by large sections of the population has come to be defined as unacceptable and unnecessary. We are no longer prepared to put up with the vicissitudes of our day-to-day existence if these have an adverse effect on our mental state. We have come to believe that we have a right to positive mental health and that anything which stands in the way of this objective should be and can be overcome. Although by no means everyone will couch this belief in these terms, there is good evidence that this kind of change has occurred (Robertson and Cochrane 1976).

The next stage concerns the recognition that some form of external help is required. The alternative here is to resort to self-medication with alcohol or other drugs which are readily available, or perhaps to engage in what is sometimes known as antidepressive behaviour. This may mean, for example, keeping busy with more cheerful things, not allowing oneself time to brood on one's problems, counting one's blessings and a whole host of other activities which some people may have and may use to reduce the need to seek help from other people.

Even after the need for external help is recognized it is still not inevitable that this help will be sought from a doctor. Many people avoid seeing their general practitioner wherever possible, either because they are fearful of the outcome of such an encounter or because they believe they might be thought to be 'wasting the doctor's time'. In any case many people have a more or less extended network of social contacts who may be able to offer useful help or guidance. Other professional help such as that available from priests may also be sought in preference to that of a doctor.

When visiting the doctor many people believe they must present some physical symptoms for him to consider, even though the real basis of their illness might be psychological. It is also the case that many genuine physical symptoms have psychogenic origins. This can and does lead to failure by the doctor to recognize the true origin of his patient's problems. Goldberg and Huxley (1980), for example, have evidence to show that doctors are less likely to consider a patient to be suffering from a psychological problem if they are male, very young or over 65, unmarried or better educated. Women and people who have been seen frequently in the recent past, together with those who are separated, divorced or widowed, are much more likely to have their illness recognized as having a psychological origin. If the doctor recognizes the problem as psychological he has a choice of whether to treat the disorder himself or to refer the patient to a psychiatrist. If he decides to treat the disorder himself he may or may not arrive at a diagnosis of depression and subsequently he may or may not offer appropriate medications. It may be the case, for example, that a middle-aged woman suffering from depression will be offered minor tranquillizers such as Valium and Librium rather than antidepressive medications.

The psychiatrist, who will usually see the patient in the context of a mental hospital, will have the option of confirming or not confirming the general practitioner's decision that the illness of his patient has a psychological basis. Further, the psychiatrist may or may not decide that any psychological illness which does exist is evidence of depression. Finally, the psychiatrist has available a variety of forms of treatment ranging from full-time inpatient care in a mental hospital to very occasional outpatient contact once every six months or even less frequently.

At each stage of the process outlined in Fig. 1 it is obvious that the social characteristics of the potential patient will play a part in forming his or her decision. Someone who has a great number of friends may find less need to go to the doctor; women may find it easier to complain of symptoms than men; on the other hand, men may have more alternative forms of deviance available to them (such as heavy drinking) rather than seeking professional advice; psychiatrists may be influenced by the status characteristics of the patients they are confronted with in deciding what to do with them; and the availability of various treatment resources will also have an influence on their decision regarding the disposal of the patient.

Plan of the book

We have arrived at three basic propositions which will inform the subsequent development of this book throughout the remaining chapters. *First*, there is the notion that different social groups are more or less vulnerable to the onset of mental illness because of their social characteristics. *Second*, social characteristics will also largely determine the way in which people respond to the psychological problems they experience. *Third*, the likely effectiveness of the various ways people have of coping with the ravages of psychological distress will also be influenced by social characteristics.

The next four chapters are each devoted to one of the major social status variables which have been shown to influence the likelihood of psychological disorder in Britain. Chapter 6 deals specifically with stress which it is proposed to use as the major intervening variable by which social statuses are translated into individual psychological problems. The particular example of unemployment will be used as illustrating the advantages and disadvantages of stress-based models of psychopathology.

The leading alternative to the individual medical model of mental illness is discussed in Chapter 7 and the evidence in favour of this approach is evaluated.

The final chapter is devoted to an extension of some of the points made in this introductory chapter which will be elaborated in the light of the information reviewed in the intervening chapters. A model of the way in which people respond to the occurrence of stress, given their social resources, will be developed which, while it will not offer an exhaustive account of the occurrence of all mental illness, will try to encompass what is known of the variations in the incidence of mental illness across different social groups.

Chapter 2

Social class differences

Probably one of the first relationships observed between social variables and individual psychological disorder was that between social class and schizophrenia. Indeed, it is from the continuing examination of this particular relationship that many of the other social variables that influence psychological status have emerged. Since the original studies in the 1930s in the USA there has been a tremendous number of follow-up investigations conducted all over the world. The results of all these studies show a surprising degree of consistency but we are hardly any closer to resolving the problem of explaining these findings than were the authors of the original researches. In this chapter we will look briefly at the major approaches to the study of the relationship between social class and mental illness and then examine each of the explanations that has been offered for the observed relationship in turn. The mass of evidence available is far too great to be exhaustively reviewed, and in any case has been thoroughly examined elsewhere (especially in Dohrenwend and Dohrenwend 1969).

The ecological approach

The original study mentioned above was that of Faris

and Dunham which was published in 1939. They
plotted the addresses of all patients admitted with
mental disorders to four state and eight private hospitals in Chicago for a twelve-year period on a census
map of that city. When the rate of mental illness was expressed in terms of cases per 100,000 of population
they saw a very great range of incidence across the
different districts of the city. This was particularly
noticeable for schizophrenia, where the rate ranged
from over 700 cases per 100,000 adults in city-centre
districts to well under 100 cases per 100,000 in the
peripheral residential districts. The next step was to
correlate other demographic and social indices with
the differential rates of mental hospital admission
found in the various districts of Chicago. Areas from
which large numbers of patients came were also found
to have high rates of alcoholism, drug abuse, poverty
and to have a skewed social class distribution such that
the lowest social classes were considerably overrepresented. These were also the 'disorganized' areas of the
city with high levels of social mobility, a high proportion of foreign-born residents, a large proportion of
the population living in single rooms or in hostels, a
high proportion of the unmarried and a high proportion of people living below the official poverty
level. Faris and Dunham were quick to seize upon the
explanation that poverty and social disorganization
were instrumental in producing schizophrenia and other
psychological problems. As this was one of the original
studies in psychiatric epidemiology the authors can
perhaps be forgiven for making several fundamental
errors which later studies have been able to avoid.

The first of these is the so called ecological fallacy.
This refers to the danger of extrapolating from the
ecological characteristics of an area to the individuals
who come from that area. Just because a particular
district may have, let us say, a high proportion of people living alone this does not mean that any individual

case from that district will be experiencing social isolation. It may be that a particular individual is living in a well-integrated family but happens to live in a relatively poor district of the city. In other words, individual characteristics can be determined only by an examination of individual cases and not of social aggregates. Faris and Dunham's study yielded no direct evidence that the individuals who were admitted to mental hospitals had in fact experienced poverty and social disorganization.

The second problem stems from the inevitable methodological weakness of relying on a study of institutionalized cases only. It would by no means be incompatible with the basic findings of Faris and Dunham's study if it were discovered that there were almost as many cases of psychological disorder in the better-off, more integrated areas of the city but that these were looked after in a different way. Perhaps it was the social disorganization of the inner-city areas which meant that people had to resort to institutional care when in other areas of the city they might be taken care of at home or by local doctors. A related point is the possible bias caused by using the home address of the patient at the time of committal to a mental hospital as being indicative of the address of the patient during the onset of the disorder. Obviously, if the social environment is believed to have aetiological significance in the production of mental illness then it must be the environment in which the person was living prior to the development of that illness that is subjected to examination. It is feasible that the patients who Faris and Dunham believed lived in the socially disorganized areas of Chicago had in fact moved there relatively recently – prior to admission to hospital but after the onset of their disorder.

This brings up the most significant of all the problems of explanation generated by this study, namely the direction of causality. At the time the authors were

thoroughly convinced that the factors of poverty and
social disorganization were contributing to the development of mental illness. It has become very apparent
since that it is equally plausible to posit a direction of
causality entirely opposite to that initially assumed. As
Dunham admitted a long time after the original study
'...our findings, while consistent with the notion that
poor people tend to become schizophrenic, were no
less consistent with the almost diametrically opposite
notion that schizophrenic people tend to become
poor'. (Dunham 1977: 62, in Cockerham 1981: 173).
The debate about whether low social class position is
causative of psychological disorder or vice versa has
raged ever since the original study was done and is still
not completely resolved.

The Faris and Dunham study has been treated in
some detail as it is of great importance in the history
of psychiatric epidemiology. However, in many senses
it represented something of a dead end because the
ecological approach has not since proved to be very
fruitful. The reasons for the decline in the use of this
approach should be apparent from the criticisms made
of this particular study.

Studies of individual patients admitted to mental hospitals

The most obvious logical solution to many of these
methodological difficulties is to look more closely at
the characteristics of individuals admitted to mental
hospital. Many such studies have in fact been carried
out both in the United States and in Britain. They
allow a much more flexible analysis of the data to be
undertaken because far more information is gleaned
for each individual case than the ecological method
can ever hope to supply.

Hollingshead and Redlich (1958) looked at all the
people in New Haven, Connecticut who were receiving

any formal psychiatric care between June and December 1950. They assigned each patient to a social class on the basis of an index made up of occupational and educational level. As Table 1 clearly shows, there was a strong relationship between social class and patient status. Patients were considerably underrepresented in the business, professional and managerial classes as well as in white-collar occupations. Their distribution approached that of the general population in social class IV which was comprised of semi-skilled factory workers and was double the proportion of the non-patient population who were in the semi-skilled and unskilled worker category (V). This trend was accentuated even further when only the most seriously disturbed, schizophrenic patients were considered. Further, Hollingshead and Redlich found that many other factors to do with treatment, course and duration of the disorder were related to social class in a similar way.

Table 1 Percentage of patients and non-patients in each social class in New Haven, Connecticut, 1950

Social Class	Non-patients	Patients	Non-patient: patient ratio
I and II (business; professional; managerial)	11.4	8.0	0.70
III (white collar)	20.4	13.7	0.66
IV (semi-skilled manual)	49.8	40.1	0.81
V (unskilled manual)	18.4	38.2	2.08

Source: Adapted from Hollingshead and Redlich 1958

These findings were further reinforced ten years later when Myers and Bean (1968) traced the patients who had formed the original sample in 1950. They found clear evidence that the patients' social class status in 1950 was predictive of their psychological status and their social adjustment ten years later in 1960. Patients who had originated in higher social classes were less likely still to be hospitalized, more likely to be receiving outpatient care and less likely to have died in the intervening decade than patients from lower social classes. Indeed, a good proportion of patients from lower social class backgrounds had not been discharged from hospital at any period during the decade 1950 to 1960.

Similar patterns in the relationship of social class and mental illness based on mental hospital admission data have been found in Britain, too. Table 2 shows some of the results from a complex study carried out in Aberdeen in the 1960s by Birtchnell (1971) using the Registrar-General's classification of social classes which for all practical purposes is similar to that used by Hollingshead and Redlich. Birtchnell found that patients were overrepresented in social classes IV (semi-skilled manual workers) and V (unskilled manual workers). Again he found that this was much more marked for psychotic patients – mainly schizophrenics – than for the total group of patients. As is shown in Table 2, while there are about 50 per cent more patients from social class V than would be expected given the class distribution of the population, there are 128 per cent more psychotic patients in this group than

Table 2 Percentage of non-patients and patients admitted to hospital in Aberdeen, 1963–67, by social class

Social class	Non-patients	All patients	Psychotic patients	Non-patient: all patients ratio	Non-patient: psychotics ratio
I	5.5	5.0	4.3	0.91	0.78
II	21.0	19.7	15.4	0.94	0.73
III	46.8	35.9	27.0	0.77	0.58
IV	17.8	25.4	31.9	1.43	1.79
V	9.0	14.1	20.5	1.57	2.28

Source: Adapted from Birtchnell 1971

would be expected. We will return to the work of Hollingshead and Redlich and that of Birtchnell when we consider possible explanations for these findings.

Community survey studies of the epidemiology of psychological disorder

Since the mid-1950s growing use has been made of the community survey to examine the relationship between sociodemographic variables and psychological distress. The reasons for this are fairly obvious in that the community survey allows a much more detailed and intensive analysis of the possible causes of psychological disorder to be undertaken than does either the ecological method or the analysis of the characteristics of patients receiving treatment. The major problem with community surveys is the measurement of the central dependant variable, in this case psychological disorder. As most surveys are conducted by lay interviewers, it is usually necessary to have a standardized measure of the existence of psychological symptoms which can either be used mechanically by the interviewer or can even be self-administered by the respondent. The usual approach taken in developing such an instrument is to take as a basis those psychological symptoms which most clearly differentiate between people diagnosed as mentally ill and those who are not so diagnosed. This was the method used for validating the Langner 22 Item Index which is probably the most widely used of all the measures (Langner 1962). As it will be so frequently referred to in the following pages a copy of the instrument is included as Appendix I. This list of twenty-two psychological symptoms which are scored as present or absent for each respondent was developed during the so-called Midtown Manhattan survey carried out by Srole and Langner and their associates (Srole *et al.*

1961; Langner and Michael 1962). These twenty-two symptoms were found to be the most powerful in discriminating between mental hospital patients and individuals diagnosed as psychologically well, after a clinical interview with a psychiatrist. The Midtown study was one of the first large-scale surveys of psychological impairment in the community, and it has been used as a model for many subsequent investigations. The report from this study is contained in three very large volumes so obviously only the briefest résumé is possible here. What the investigators did was to contact a random sample of the non-institutionalized adult population of Manhattan, New York. Each person was interviewed extensively at home and data were collected on demographic variables, social status, experiences of stress, psychological symptoms and a wide variety of other psychometric measures. Each interview schedule was subsequently read independently by two psychiatrists who rated each individual on a zero to six rating scale of mental health. This scale was subsequently collapsed to a zero-to-three scale of psychological impairment. For our purposes the major results of this study are shown in Table 3.

Table 3　Percentage of community survey respondents in each mental health category by social class in New York, 1954

| | Social class | | |
Mental health rating	Upper	Middle	Lower
Well	34.1	21.4	12.9
Mild symptoms	35.5	38.1	39.6
Moderate symptoms	20.5	23.7	27.7
Psychiatrically impaired	9.9	16.8	19.8

Source:　Adapted from Srole *et al* 1961

Note first of all the extraordinarily high proportion of the total sample of people interviewed who were considered by the psychiatrists who made the ratings to have some psychological impairment. Only about 25 per cent of the respondents in this study were given a clean bill of health by the psychiatrists. The largest proportion were considered to have some mild symptom formation or moderate symptoms. We find, as is to be expected, a marked social class influence on the proportions of people with and without symptoms. Whereas in the highest social class group there are almost four times as many people considered to be well as psychiatrically impaired, in the lowest social class group there are almost twice as many ill people as there are people diagnosed as well.

Turning finally to a recent study of psychological health in the community in Britain, Cochrane and Stopes-Roe (1980a), using the Langner Index, found a very similar pattern (Table 4). Using three broad social class groupings it was found that there was a linear relationship between social status and number of symptoms reported. Those in non-manual occupations had on average about three symptoms while those in unskilled manual occupations approached an average of five symptoms.

Table 4 Average number of psychological symptoms reported by different social classes in England

Social class	No.	Mean	Standard deviation
Non-manual	60	3.10	3.30
Skilled manual/supervisory	112	3.74	3.82
Semi-skilled and unskilled manual	60	4.88	3.74

Source: From Cochrane and Stopes-Roe 1980a

Thus it is clear that in whichever way the evidence is gathered, and whatever index of psychological ill health is used, the findings are consistent that lower social status is associated with a higher risk of psychological problems. In a comparative survey of forty-four studies using the community survey method,

Dohrenwend and Dohrenwend (1969) found that social class was the only demographic variable that was consistently related to psychological status. Age, sex and race showed no such consistent relationship. In twenty-eight of the thirty-three studies which used social class as a variable there was more psychological disturbance in the lowest social class than in any of the others.

We must now turn to the problems of explaining these findings.

Explanations of the social class/mental illness relationship

Some of the possible explanations of the relationship have been alluded to above. Faris and Dunham assumed that social status was causal of psychological status, but it was pointed out that the opposite was equally plausible. These two hypotheses have come to be known as the social causation and the social selection hypotheses respectively.

Social causation hypothesis

This category of explanation postulates that social class is correlated with a large number of other variables which might contribute to a higher rate of psychological disturbance in the lower social groups. Some of the characteristics of lower social class life which have been suggested as possible intervening variables are an excess of stress, poor working conditions, lack of control over the environment, lower educational level, and the familial transmission of values.

The single factor which has received most attention, and indeed which may incorporate many of the other factors, is stress. It was noticed in the Midtown Manhattan study that poorer people experienced more stress in the form of poorer physical health, marital disharmony, periods of unemployment and so on, than do their richer counterparts. It is also quite possible that when these kinds of events do affect the better educated and those with a higher standard of living, they are better able to cope with the vicissitudes of stress by, for example, taking a holiday or seeking professional advice. The only other assumption that is required here is that stress is itself related to psychological ill-health. This is a common assumption and, as we shall see later, there is considerable empirical evidence to support it.

Evidence from the Midtown studies clearly supported both these assumptions (although it should be noted that the psychiatrist doing the clinical ratings had access to the stress scores for each of the respondents, thus introducing the possibility of a serious bias). It soon became apparent, however, that the relationship could not be so simple as a direct 'social class leads to more stress leads to more mental illness' model would suggest. Even when the level of stress in the different social classes was controlled it was found there was more psychological ill health in the lower social classes than in higher social classes. However, this was only true where stress was above a certain minimum level. In cases where no stress was experienced then there was very little psychological impairment in whatever class the respondent came from, but at higher levels of stress the psychological consequences seemed much more severe for those of lower than those of higher social status. In some way it appeared that the poor were less resilient to the effects of stress than were the richer people in the sample.

A major insight into the way in which social class interacts with stress to produce differential mental illness rates was provided by Phillips (1968). He looked at the distribution of *positive* experiences across the social classes as well as stressful experiences. The hypothesis was that positive or pleasant feelings might counteract the influence of stressful experiences. In his community survey of 600 people in New England, Phillips found that the occurrence of pleasant and unpleasant experiences were independent of each other: that is, they are not opposite ends of the same continuum. Although there was no noticeable social class differential in his study in the proportions of each social class reporting negative feelings (for example being upset, lonely or bored), there was a considerable social class differential in the reported experience of positive feelings. He found that more than twice as many higher social class individuals reported having a lot of positive experiences in the past month – such things as being pleased, proud, excited, interested and so on – as lower social class people. Positive experiences turned out to be the missing piece of the jigsaw as far as Phillips was concerned. Because people in the lower social classes were more likely to have high stress levels *and* the absence of positive experiences which were able to cushion the effects of stress, as it were, the relationship between social class and mental health was not obliterated when stress was controlled for. Again we see how social forces can produce conditions which increase vulnerability to mental illness.

Social selection hypothesis

The major problem with the social causation hypothesis is that a lot of the evidence available does not seem to fit. Several studies show that although the social class distribution of psychiatric patients is markedly skewed towards the lower end of the distribution, the class position of the fathers of the patients is much more normal. In other words, there is a discrepancy between the status of the patient and that of his or her family of origin. Thus, for some part of their lives at least, the patients who were in lower social class positions at the time of treatment for their illness had in fact been in a somewhat higher status group. Goldberg and Morrison (1963), for example, in their study of the social class distribution of schizophrenic patients and their fathers in England and Wales in 1956, found that although there were over twice as many patients in social class V at admission than would be expected by chance, when patients were categorized by their father's occupation at the time of the patient's birth, then they were not overrepresented at all in social class V. They concluded that 'gross social economic deprivation is unlikely to be of major aetioligical significance in schizophrenia' (Goldberg and Morrison 1963: 802). Findings such as these have led many investigators to reject the social causation hypothesis especially as it applies to schizophrenia, also in respect of some other psychological disorders, and substitute what has come to be known as the social selection or 'drift' hypothesis. The drift hypothesis was first described by Myerson (1941). It is an attempt to explain the concentration of patients in the lower social classes as being a result of the inability of people with psychiatric disorders to maintain the socioeconomic position of their family of origin. Thus psychiatric impairment is considered to influence social status rather than the other way round.

Since Myerson's original formulation in terms of intergenerational downward social mobility, many other varieties of the drift hypothesis have been developed. If, for example, a genetic component in some disorders such as schizophrenia is posited then the drift could be across many generations. The accumulation of psychotic individuals in the lowest social groups might not be marked by a great deal of downward social mobility between any two generations but over long periods of history it could account for the excess in the lower social strata. Schizophrenia, and perhaps depression, certainly does have some genetic contribution. The extent to which genetic influences are necessary or sufficient for the development of these conditions is still unclear. However, it will probably be necessary to incorporate a genetic component into any satisfactory explanation of the social class correlation with psychiatric disturbance.

More limited intergenerational downward social mobility could account for the higher numbers of psychiatrically ill people in the lower social classes without invoking any general hypothesis. It is not hard to see, for example, how schizophrenia may so disable a person that whatever social class they happen to be born into they are unable to maintain the class position of their parents. Thus they would, in occupational terms at least, end up occupying perhaps the lowest rung on the status ladder. This was certainly the conclusion of Goldberg and Morrison and is supported by several other studies such as those of Birtchnell (1971) who extended the analysis from schizophrenia to most other psychiatric disorders with the exception of neurotic patients. Gerrard and Houston (1953), in an ecological level study of schizophrenics in Worcester, Massachusetts, found that the greatest proportion of the excess of schizophrenics who came from poor areas of the city was removed if recent arrivals in these areas were excluded. In other words, although a lot of schizophrenics were admitted from poor areas they had not lived there all their lives but had moved there, probably since the onset of their illness. Such areas may offer the kind of accommodation (hostels, lodging houses) that the seriously disturbed person either seeks out or can afford.

The drift downwards in social status may also occur within the lifetime of an individual: although the person destined to become psychiatrically impaired commences his career at a level equivalent to, or perhaps even exceeding, that of his family of origin, his disabilities prevent him from maintaining that position and produce a subsequent drift downwards. Dunham (1965) in his study of psychiatric patients in Detroit found that a distinguishing feature of male schizophrenics was a much lower occupational level than their educational achievements would have predicted. It is frequently observed that the onset of schizophrenia often occurs in late adolescence, after formal education is finished but before a person has got underway in his career.

The final, and perhaps most convincing, version of the drift hypothesis takes cognizance of the fact that for the greater part of this century at least the normal pattern has not been one of status similarity between generations. What most Western societies have witnessed is a progressive shrinking of the lowest social classes in relative terms as industrial techniques have replaced many of the jobs that formerly made up this social category. Despite this contraction relatively low levels of unemployment have been maintained because of an equivalent expansion in skilled manual and non-manual occupations. Thus in the mid-1960s in Britain only 27 per cent of the sons of unskilled manual workers were themselves in that category, most (nearly 40 per cent) had moved into skilled manual occupations. The reverse, however, was not true; the sons of skilled manual workers had either remained in that category or had themselves been upwardly mobile (Sergeant 1972: 82). If the typical pattern is for upward mobility out of the lowest social class group, then it is possible for an excess of psychologically disturbed individuals to build up in that group if they are the individuals who fail to achieve upward social mobility when it is the norm. In other words, the psychiatrically impaired people form an increasing part of the residue in this group. There is more than a little evidence to support this view. The major study was undertaken by Turner and Wagenfeld (1967). They found no evidence that the 200 schizophrenic patients they interviewed were downwardly socially mobile compared to their fathers, but they did find that they were less upwardly socially mobile than a comparable group of non-patients. The patients had not achieved as high an occupational level as most people of their social class background. A much more extensive study has been reported recently by Harkey, Miles and Rushing (1976). They took a global concept of 'behavioral dysfunction' as their dependant variable and related it to socioeconomic status as measured by income. Their results strongly supported the hypothesis that behavioural dysfunctions were causal of low income rather than the reverse. They found that the primary effect of behavioural dysfunctions was to retard upward social mobility rather than to cause downward mobility. This effect was apparently strongest in young adulthood when the person was looking for his or her first job. We can probably assume, therefore, that the failure to achieve the expected degree of upward social mobility is not confined to schizophrenics but may also occur as a result of less severe psychological disorders.

It must be pointed out that even in the Turner and Wagenfeld study there was still an excess of schizophrenics in the lowest social status group even after the failure to achieve upward social mobility was controlled for. Similarly Dunham's (1965) study, and indeed most of those that support one or other versions of the drift hypothesis, are not consistent with the idea that drift is the entire explanation for the excessive morbidity in the lowest social class group. This has led to attempts either to combine the causation and drift models or to attempts to assess their relative contribution to the relationship between social class and mental illness.

Lee (1976) specifically compared the two explanations in a reanalysis of a study of the psychological symptom levels of 130 members of rural communities in Canada. He found some evidence for both models (i.e. symptom levels were probably elevated by economic deprivation as well as the failure of those people with psychiatric problems to achieve as high a status as they might otherwise have done) but concluded that the social causation model was more plausible than the drift hypothesis.

A crucial test of the two explanations?

In their 1969 review of studies in this area, Dohrenwend and Dohrenwend suggested what they called 'a crucial test' to determine the relative contributions of the social causation and social selection hypotheses in explaining the relationship between social class and psychiatric disorder. The design they suggest involves adding a third variable to this relationship which would operate to increase the magnitude of the relationship if one of the hypotheses were correct and decrease it if the other were correct. The variable suggested by the Dohrenwends which would operate in this way is membership of a minority and disadvantaged ethnic group.

If the social causation hypothesis is valid it would be expected that, at any given level of social class, members of a disadvantaged minority group would show more psychiatric disturbance than members of the majority group. The reason for this is that membership of an ethnic minority would act in a way analogous to the alleged effect of low social class; that is, the effects of minority status and socioeconomic status would be additive. Those of higher social class would still have the 'burden' of minority group status to contend with while those of lower social class would be doubly disadvantaged compared to their counterparts in the advantaged ethnic majority.

On the other hand, if the social selection hypothesis is correct the effects of prejudice and discrimination against minority group members would reverse the

		Ethnic group	
		Advantaged	Disadvantaged
Social class	High	2 1	1 2
	Low	4 3	2 4

Fig. 2   Rank order of four status groups for psychological disorder
(1 = lowest rate, 4 = highest rate) predicted by two explanatory
models

The predicted rank orders generated by the social selection model
are above the diagonals and those predicted by the social causation
model are below the diagonals.

Source: Adapted from Dohrenwend and Dohrenwend 1969: 56

prediction. The lower social class among the ethnic
majority would contain a disproportionate number of
psychologically impaired people who had filtered
down the hierarchy (or failed to be upwardly mobile)
because of psychological problems, but the equivalent
social class group among the ethnic minority could be
expected to contain a high proportion of stable, well-
adjusted people who were trapped in their lowly status
position because of racial or ethnic discrimination.
These people would sufficiently dilute the mixture in
this group so that the average level of psychological
disturbance would be *lower* than in the equivalent low
status group in the ethnic majority. The same argument can be applied to the higher status groupings in
both ethnic groups: because those individuals who had
achieved or maintained high status had been much
more rigidly selected in the ethnic minority than had

their ethnically advantaged peers, we would again expect to find a lower level of symptoms in the ethnic minority than in the ethnic majority controlling for social status. The predictions from this design are summarized in Fig. 2.

This design is unusually attractive in psychiatric epidemiology because it does make clearly contrasting predictions on the basis of the two models. However, results based on this design have not lived up to expectation. In the original study by the Dohrenwends, conducted in New York, they compared Negroes, Puerto Ricans and an advantaged white group (those of Jewish and Irish origin). Using income as an index of social status, it turned out that Puerto Ricans as a group had a higher level of psychological disorder than did the white group when matched for social class, but blacks, however, had a lower level of psychiatric disorder than did whites. Thus the results of the comparison of Puerto Ricans and whites clearly supported the social causation hypothesis while the black/white comparison apparently supported the social selection hypothesis.

The picture was even more confused when a similar study was undertaken in Britain by Cochrane and Stopes-Roe (1981b), using Pakistani and Indian immigrants as the disadvantaged ethnic groups. They found that the usual social class gradient in psychological disorder only occurred in native whites and did not apply at all to either group of first generation Asian immigrants. However, as the Asian immigrants tended to have lower levels of symptoms in each social class grouping than did the natives, Cochrane and Stopes-Roe concluded that their study provided more support for the social selection hypothesis than the social causation hypothesis.

On only one occasion has the Dohrenwends' crucial test provided a clearcut answer to the original question. Antunes *et al.* (1974) looked at the level of psychological symptoms among blacks, Mexican Americans and white Anglo-Saxon Americans matched for social class in Houston, Texas. In this study the results clearly supported the social selection hypothesis because both blacks and Mexicans had lower symptom levels than did the Anglo-Saxons in each social group, despite the extra disadvantages of being members of ethnic minorities.

Thus, while the Dohrenwends' design has not really yet provided the crucial test it promised between the two hypotheses, the weight of the evidence seems to be swinging towards social selection rather than social causation as making the largest contribution to the explanation of the high rates of psychological problems in low social class groups.

An attempt at integration – Kohn's model

Kohn (1968, 1972) has attempted to integrate a large number of the findings from the studies of social class and psychological disorder into one explanatory model. His formulation was specifically developed to account for the relationship between class and schizophrenia but there is no reason why it cannot be extended to account for the similar relationships observed between social class and other forms of psychological disorder.

The generalized version of Kohn's model begins by accepting that there is probably a genetic contribution to many forms of psychological disorder. The evidence of a genetic contribution is strongest for schizophrenia but has also been suggested for alcoholism, anxiety reaction, obsessionality and paranoid reactions (Slater and Roth 1969; Martin 1977). To the extent that there is an inherited component in these psychological disorders, Kohn argues, there must have been higher rates of the disorder among the ancestors of the current generation of patients. The disabling effect of the disorders on earlier generations would have produced downward social mobility and this process of multi-generational drift would contribute to the increased proportion of disturbed people in the lower echelons of society. However, heredity factors cannot be considered a sufficient condition for the development of a psychological illness. Many, perhaps most, people who have some genetic predisposition do not become psychologically disturbed and some others without predisposition do experience periods of mental illness.

The second element in Kohn's tripartite model is stress. As we shall see in a subsequent chapter, there is considerable evidence that the occurrence of stress is consistently related to the onset of psychological disorders. Again, however, the magnitude of the relationship is not large. It is estimated that only about 10 per cent of the variability in psychological state between people can be accounted for by their stress experiences (Cochrane and Sobol 1980). While it is certainly true that people from lower social classes do experience more stress, this can hardly be a complete explanation. This has been ruled out on empirical grounds by the studies of Langner and Michael and of Phillips, discussed earlier. It is clear that at any given level of stress those of lower social status are more prone to psychiatric disorder than those of higher social status.

The third and final element proposed by Kohn is the familial transmission of 'conceptions of reality'. There seem to be considerable social class differences in the values that are transmitted from one generation to the next.

> The lower a man's social class position, the more likely he is to value conformity to external authority and to believe that such conformity is all that his own capacities and the exigencies of the world allow; in particular the lower a man's social class position, the more likely is his orientational system to be marked by a rigid

conservative view of man and his social institutions, fearfulness and distrust, and a fatalistic belief that one is at the mercy of forces and people beyond one's control, often beyond one's understanding. (Kohn 1972: 300)

Hess (1970) gives a detailed account of the way in which the psychological structure of poorer people is influenced by their experience of powerlessness. The poor have little or no economic power, little social influence and none of the power and confidence that knowledge brings. They are repeatedly exposed to situations in which their lack of power is brought home to them. For example, as children they experience demands for compliance and obedience from their fathers; at school the situation is similar and in later life the jobs available usually entail following instructions rather than giving them and, what is more, these instructions are typically meaningless in the context in which they are given. The poor person is much more susceptible to having his life affected by people and events beyond his control. He has much less control over his job, his house, where he lives and his life style than his middle-class counterpart. Although Hess was more concerned with intellectual development than with psychological wellbeing, his analysis has an important implication for this area as well. He suggests that a common adaptive reaction to the social situation of powerlessness is to adopt attitudes of low self-esteem, dependency and passivity. Children with such parents will learn to be apathetic and relatively help-less when they encounter stress in later life. They will not have acquired the necessary flexibility of adaptive responses that their middle-class peers will have acquired.

Kohn brings the three factors of genetic vulnerability, social stress, and value systems together. He predicts that the probability of psychological disorder will be highest when these three elements occur in the same individual. Each of these elements separately is more likely to occur in the lower social classes and together their occurrence is considerably more frequent in that location. A person may experience a large amount of stress but if he does not have genetic vulnerability and a rigid and narrow conception of social reality and a poor sense of personal efficacy then he will not succumb to the stress and will avoid psychological disturbance. Equally a person with the latter two characteristics but who is not subjected to high levels of stress may never manifest any psychological problems.

Although Kohn's model is not yet completely worked out, and has not been tested thoroughly in empirical studies, it does begin to articulate a lot of the evidence from the disparate studies reviewed in this chapter. It entails a clear recognition that relationships between social and psychological variables are bound to entail a complex interaction rather than being the result of a simple and direct flow of cause and effect.

Chapter 3

Sex differences in psychological wellbeing

Possibly even better known than the social class differentials in recorded rates of mental illness are the sex differences. In Britain, as in several other countries, women are very considerably overrepresented among mental hospital patients. Although the higher rate of mental illness for women has been recorded for some time, the increased attention paid recently to sexual inequality in society has led to a refocusing of attention on this issue. If there is a causal relationship between the two variables of sex and mental illness then the direction of causality must be from the former to the latter. Unlike the social class relationship, there is no way in which psychological status can influence gender. This is not to say that the relationship must be a causal one but whatever the relationship, sex must be the prior variable.

Overall about 40 per cent more women than men are admitted for treatment in mental hospitals in England every year. Figures published by the Department of Health and Social Security (DHSS) show that the differential rate of admission for the sexes is not spread evenly over all diagnostic categories. An examination of Table 5 shows that in the case of schizophrenia, for example, the sexes have more or less similar rates of mental hospital admission. The largest

Table 5 Rates of admission to mental hospitals in England in 1977 per 100,000 population by sex and diagnostic group

Diagnosis	Males	Females	Excess of female over male rate (%)
All diagnoses	315	439	+ 39
Schizophrenia and related	64	62	− 3
Depressive psychoses	31	65	+ 109
Other psychoses	23	37	+ 61
Alcoholic psychoses + alcoholism	39	15	− 62
Drug dependence	4	2	− 50
Psychoneuroses	30	63	+ 110
Personality and behaviour disorders	37	42	+ 14
Other conditions*	87	153	+ 76

Source: Adapted from DHSS 1980
* This category includes depression not specified as neurotic or psychotic

sex differences are in the two categories which contain patients admitted with a diagnosis of depression. In the 'depressive psychosis' category women are twice as likely to be admitted as men and in the 'psycho-neuroses' category the same pattern emerges. It should be noted that this category includes those diagnosed as neurotically depressed. In the 'other conditions' category, too, women are overrepresented, and as 'depression' not specified by the admitting psychiatrist as neurotic or psychotic is put into this category this probably accounts for a large part of the female excess. In those diagnostic categories where men are overre-presented, such as alcohol psychosis and drug depen-dence, the total numbers of admissions are quite small and do not compensate for the overrepresentation of women in the larger categories. Obviously, then, the major difference between the sexes appears to be the very high rate of depression recorded among women.

Before proceeding to an examination of possible

causes of these differences two other points are worth considering. Although not revealed in Table 5, there is a very significant age-related pattern of admissions which also distinguishes the sexes. In the youngest age groups males have conspicuously higher treatment rates than do females. After the age of about 15, however, the female excess over males becomes large and consistent. Both these phenomena, the high rates of depression among women and the age reversal, have also been reported in the United States (Gove 1972).

Table 6   Rates of admission to mental hospital per 100,000 population by sex and marital status, England and Wales, 1973

Marital status	Males	Females	Ratio M : F
Single	663	623	0.93
Married	257	433	1.68
Widowed	752	720	0.96
Divorced	1,959	1,596	0.81
Married : single ratio	0.39	0.70	

Source: Adapted from Cochrane and Stopes-Roe 1981c

Equally dramatic, and perhaps better known, is the enormous influence that marital status has on mental hospitalization rates. In general, being married is associated with a much lower risk of being recorded as mentally ill. Those at highest risk are the divorced and widowed, with the 'never married' falling somewhere between the married and the previously married. The figures for mental hospital admissions broken down by sex and marital status in Table 6 show, however, that the marital status variation in rates of mental hospital admission is different for the two sexes. The difference in rates between the married and the unmarried is much smaller for women than for men. In other words, although married women have substantially lower rates of mental hospital admission than do single women, marriage seems to afford them less protection, as it were, than it does to men. In fact, single women have lower rates of mental illness than do single men, and the same is true of widowed and divorced women compared to men of the same status. It is only in the married category, which of course accounts for the majority of the adult population, that women have higher rates of mental hospital admission than do men. It is worth repeating, however, that even for women the married are less at risk of mental hospital admission than is any other marital status category.

Here, as in the case of other social variables, it is dangerous to rely exclusively on recorded mental hospital admissions as the data base for inferring substantial differences. However, other indices of psychological status (such as outpatient, day patient, emergency and domiciliary visits from psychiatrists, consultation with general practitioners and the results of community surveys) all point in the same direction – women do have more psychological problems than do men. This in itself is quite unusual because in almost every other form of deviance that is systematically recorded, men outnumber women quite considerably. Thus in crime, vandalism, drunkenness, drug abuse, sexual deviance, all forms of violence and even suicide, men outnumber women. A case could be made out that it is all a question of definition when it comes to considering sex differences. If all deviance was aggregated into a global measure then men would certainly appear the more deviant of the two sexes. It happens that we have taken as our topic of interest the form of deviance labelled as mental illness, and this, perhaps, is the unique category in which women are more prominent than men.

Explanations of sex differences in mental illness

Given that sex differences in psychiatric disorder are real and not an artefact of over-reliance on inpatient statistics, and for the moment putting aside the problem of the definition of deviant categories, what are the most likely explanations for the recorded differences? There are two fairly obvious types of explanation which will be considered in turn: the biological basis of sex differences; and the sex roles prescribed by our society for men and women. There is, however, a third explanation which is perhaps less obvious but has attracted a great deal of attention recently. This is an explanation provoked by the observation of the marital status differentials in mental illness already commented on. A hypothesis has been developed based on the different meaning of being married for men and women.

Biological explanations

The most widely accepted popular explanation for sex differences in mental illness is that women are innately more emotional than men and more prone to emotional upsets. At first glance this is an attractive proposition because quite probably there are differences between the emotional responsiveness of men and women at any particular point in time. However, for an explanation to be truly biological the difference between the sexes should be invariant over time and show consistency across different social groups. Ultimately, too, some sex-linked mechanism for the basis of the biological differences would have to be demonstrated. On all of these points the biological explanation for sex differences seems to be inadequate.

Although various mechanisms which may cause sex differences in psychological state, particularly depression, have been suggested – such as premenstrual tension, postpartum depression, the menopause, and even the use of oral contraceptives – these in fact are very unlikely to account for the large differences found in the rates of mental illness between the two sexes. In the most thorough, recent review of biological agents which could possibly influence depression Weissman and Klerman (1977) concluded that 'while some portion of the sex differences in depression, probably during the childbearing years, may be explained endocrinologically, this factor is not sufficient to account for the large differences'. They found, for example, that the effect of the menopause on psychological state was itself socially mediated. Women were led to believe that the menopause may be associated with emotional upsets and this became a self-fulfilling prophecy. There is no hard evidence that the menopause produces a direct effect on psychological functioning.

The fact that the observed sex differences in mental health are far from universal across time and place also seriously weakens any explanation based on biological differences between the sexes. Although reliable runs of figures over a long time-period are not readily available, it appears that the excess of female over male rates of mental hospital admissions is a relatively recent phenomenon. Lowe and Garratt (1959) cite figures which show that early this century men were somewhat more likely to be admitted to mental hospital than women and that substantially higher female rates have only been recorded since the Second World War. Equally there are societies, and indeed ethnic groups within our own society, where the pattern is reversed and in fact men have higher rates of mental illness than do women. This is true in the Republic of Ireland and in Scotland. Most important of all however is the sex/marital status interaction in rates of illness illustrated in Table 6. It is difficult to see how a major biological difference between the two sexes in the susceptibility to mental illness could have appeared only recently, only in certain ethnic groups, and only

in the married. Obviously any kind of biological explanation must be placed firmly in a social context for it
to be able to provide a useful explanation for differences in mental illness.

Sex role definitions of men and women

There are a number of factors in the different roles
created by society for men and women, and indeed in
the power relationships between the two sexes, which
may provide a sounder explanation for sex differences
in psychological disturbance.

Sex discrimination has recently become a very well
documented and researched phenomenon in Western
societies. It is certainly true that in many areas of
employment (job opportunities, relative remuneration
and promotion prospects, for example) and in personal
relationships, women are often at a disadvantage compared to men. It would be surprising indeed if this
institutionalized inequality produced by social definition did not exact a psychological price upon the inferior group. This is especially true when the dominant
cultural values assert the importance of independence
and achievement in assigning status even though the
opportunities for these achievements may in fact be
limited by institutional arrangements.

Probably just as important as the direct effects of sex
discrimination on mental health, however, are the
equally powerful effects of the sex role definition
which underlie these structural inequalities. Traditional sex role definitions are based on the notion of
complementarity between men and women: for example, men are supposed to be dominant and women are
supposed to be submissive. However, it is obvious
from even a cursory examination of the traits traditionally considered appropriate for men and women
that the assignment of these traits has not been without
bias.

Since men hold the power and authority, women are rewarded for developing a set of psychological characteristics that accommodate to and please men. Such traits – submissiveness, compliance, passivity, helplessness, weakness – have been encouraged in women and incorporated into some prevalent psychological theories in which they are defined as innate or inevitable characteristics of women. However, they are more accurately conceptualized as learned behaviors by which all subordinate group members attempt to ensure their survival . . . behaviors such as inhibition, passivity and submissiveness do not lead to favorable outcomes and play a role in the development of psychological problems. (Carmen, Russo and Miller 1981: 132l)

In a variety of contexts women who accept traditional sex role definitions will experience a relatively low capacity to influence their environment and to control their own lives. Women are more likely to be conditioned to define themselves initially in terms of their ability to attract a spouse, and subsequently to achieve their own identities vicariously through the achievements of their husbands. A woman's role and social position probably change much more on marriage than does a man's role and the psychological change may be greater too. Subsequent changes associated with motherhood, perhaps giving up employment permanently or temporarily, and in some instances geographical and social dislocation caused by husband's change of employment, may very well contribute to a condition known as 'learned helplessness'. Seligman (1975) suggested that a low capacity to influence the environment could often lead to depression. If this is the case, and there is evidence to suggest that it is, then it is easy to see how women may be more prone to this disorder than men. Should this be so then one would expect to see a decrease in the differential rates of disorder for the two sexes as women become more assertive and sex equality becomes more of a reality and consequently women achieve the degree of control over their own lives comparable to that of men.

There are two further factors associated with traditional sex role definitions that may in a sense artefactually increase the differences in mental illness rates between men and women. As it is usually considered more appropriate for women than for men to show signs of emotional distress, such as crying and comfort-seeking, it may be that women are more likely to turn to others for help with emotional problems than are men for whom this might be interpreted as a sign of weakness or inadequacy. In fact, women are indeed more likely to discuss emotional problems than men (Horwitz 1977). This being the case it would make women appear to have more psychological problems than men even though they were in fact comparable in terms of subjectively experienced symptoms of distress. When men are emotionally troubled they may turn to alternative forms of deviance such as heavy drinking, which is socially defined as a more appropriate behaviour for men than for women. This suggestion is reinforced by any examination of the drunkenness and alcoholism statistics. On the basis of this hypothesis one would expect increasing equalization in the rates of alcoholism and drunkenness with increasing sex role homogenization. However, what evidence there is at this point seems to indicate that the change in sex role behaviour (for example in employment) has gone much further than has the subjectively experienced definition of what are 'masculine' and 'feminine' characteristics (Lueptow 1980).

In this context, too, one must also be cognizant of the interpretations of symptoms made by psychiatrists and other health professionals. In a study of the attitudes of the general population towards the mentally ill and normal individuals, Jones and Cochrane (1981) asked people to rate four concepts on a series of scales, each of which was anchored by polar opposite adjectives such as 'outgoing-withdrawn', 'sensitive-insensitive', 'pleasant-unpleasant', and 'irritable-calm'. The four concepts employed were 'a mentally ill man', 'a mentally ill woman', 'a normal man', 'a normal woman'. Some of the major results of this study are referred to later but one of the subsidiary results is very important here. While the participants in this study clearly differentiated between a mentally ill man and a normal man, they saw only a much smaller dissimilarity between the concepts of a mentally ill woman and a normal woman. The concepts chosen to describe the normal man were almost diametrically opposite those chosen to describe the mentally ill man, but the characteristics of normal women were not seen as in any way the opposite of those chosen to describe the mentally ill woman. Thus it may well be that mental illness is seen as essentially a 'feminine' quality. In general men are seen as closer to the general norm of psychological health than are women. The distance to be travelled between the stereotypically normal and mentally ill behaviour is small for women and to a certain extent, therefore, this behaviour is seen as less deviant than it is for males. To the extent that mental health professionals accept the same stereotypes of sex-related differences in personality characteristics as the general population, and there is evidence that they do (Broverman *et al.* 1970), then these stereotypes may well influence the way they respond to their prospective male and female patients.

However convincing the arguments laid out above may seem to be, some powerful counter-arguments must also be recognized in any evaluation of an explanation of sex differences in mental illness based on socially generated sex role differences. As pointed out previously, there is more than a suspicion that the current excess of women over men who are psychologically impaired may be only a recent phenomenon.

There are, however, no reasons for thinking that sex role differences have become more exaggerated of late. Indeed, precisely the opposite process has been underway, even if only haltingly. It could of course be that the desire for sex equality, and the myth that it is occurring, has outstripped the actual reality of change and in a paradoxical way this has produced more stress for women rather than less.

As I have pointed out elsewhere (Cochrane and Stopes-Roe 1981c: 375) the general sex role explanation of the higher rates of mental illness among women is very much *post hoc*. An equally convincing explanation could have been developed had the figures shown more psychological problems among men. We would only need to have invoked the concepts of stress related to pressure of work, the need to be dominant, the need to provide for a family, and the need to be aggressive and assertive in personal relationships. In fact Waldron (1976) made just such a case to explain why men are more likely to die at a younger age than are women.

The failure of marriage to protect women

Neither the biological nor the general sex role explanations of the observed differences in mental hospital admissions can adequately cope with the finding that women are only more vulnerable to mental illness than men when they are married. It is perhaps worth repeating here that marriage does offer a considerable degree of protection for women in that the mental hospital admission rates for married women are substantially lower than for any category of single women, but this is much less apparent than in the case of men (see Table 6). Clearly, a complete explanation for sex differences must take account of the differential effect of marriage for men and women. An American sociologist, Walter Gove, has built an entire explanation of sex differences around the differential properties of the married state for the two sexes. Gove and his colleagues (Gove 1972; Gove 1973; Gove and Tudor 1973; Gove and Herb 1974) suggest that marriage is relatively less satisfying for women than for men and at the same time is, for many women, the sole source of their satisfaction in adult life. Whereas married men usually have two major social roles from which they may derive satisfaction – namely those of head of household and their career – women typically only have one – that of housewife. If for any reason one or other of the male's social roles fails to provide adequate satisfaction then he still has the other to fall back on for support and as a source of self-esteem. Women, on the other hand, if they are unable to derive the satisfactions they desire from being wives and mothers, are left without a viable alternative.

To compound married women's disadvantages even further, Gove suggests that the role of housewife is inevitably unstructured, invisible and of low status. As there is no material end-product and very few intrinsic or extrinsic rewards associated with housework it is consequently unlikely to provide much satisfaction to anyone. Thus a married woman is doubly disadvantaged compared to her husband who gains status from being a father and head of household without the necessity to perform the demeaning chores required of the housewife. The inadequacies of the opportunities provided for married women will have become more apparent to them as they have raised their horizons and begun to aspire to the same level of life satisfactions that are available to men.

Logically, then, Gove's model would predict that the woman most at risk of depression would be the one who is well educated, married and without a career, and whose marriage is relatively unsatisfactory. He has broadened his hypothesis somewhat so that it will also apply to the large number of married women who do in fact have jobs (a majority in this country) by adding that the jobs taken by married women are usually inherently less satisfying than the majority of men's jobs. This is because most working women are confined by sex discrimination to jobs without prospects or intrinsic rewards. In addition married women who work are also generally expected to perform the great majority of the household and childcare functions of the non-working housewife in addition to their paid employment. Gove's explanation does have a great deal to commend it. It is able to cope with two major features of the sex differences in mental hospital admission data, namely the age reversal and the marital status differential. The age reversal occurs at a time when women are approaching marriageable age and may be experiencing anticipatory socialization in the married role. With a little ingenuity it may even be stretched to cope with the chronological changes in the relative rates of mental illness. Gove suggests that since the Second World War the housewife's role has become even less fulfilling than previously because of the widespread use of labour-saving (and skill-reducing) machines in the home. Add to this the ready availability of convenience foods and other 'easy care items' and it seems that the housewife has been demoted to the status of machine minder and frozen food defroster.

The evidence

There remains very little doubt that women do in fact have higher rates of psychological disturbance than do men. We can add to the figures already cited for mental hospital admissions the results of numerous community surveys, both in the United States and in Britain. Several recent reviews of large numbers of community surveys have shown that the pattern is quite consistent whichever measures of psychological ill-health are used (Dohrenwend and Dohrenwend 1969; Goldman and Ravid 1980). The most recent large-scale community surveys in the United States and in Britain have confirmed that the pattern remains very much the same (Schwab *et al.*, 1978 in the USA; Cochrane and Stopes-Roe 1981c in Britain). Although it has been suggested that there is a trend towards a decreasing relationship between sex and mental illness (Kessler and McRae 1981), this trend is very slight indeed.

The evidence is very much less clearcut, however, on the matter of the marital status differential. Although the hospital admission figures do clearly show that marriage provides less protection for women than for men, the evidence from community surveys which in many ways are much more sensitive than mental hospital admission figures, has by no means consistently confirmed this finding. In the United States Warheit *et al.* (1976), Schwab *et al.* (1978) and Fox (1980) all found that women were more likely to have psychological problems than men in all marital status categories including the married. In England Cochrane and Stopes-Roe (1980a) in a nationwide survey could find no relationship at all between the marital status of respondents and their psychological symptom levels. Marital status did not interact with sex in the way predicted by Gove to give married women a higher score than married men on the symptom scale used.

In his analysis of various indices of mental illness in an area of Scotland, Robertson (1974) pointed out that being married may inhibit admission to hospital rather than the occurrence of psychological illnesses. This may be particularly true for married men when they have wives at home to look after them while they recover from the less serious psychological illnesses. It may be that the marital status differential in mental hospital admissions will prove to be something of a red

herring and Walter Gove's explanation based largely
on these differences may be over-elaborate.

Increasingly attention has been directed towards the
effects of paid employment for married women. Perhaps the most important evidence here comes from the
studies of Brown and Harris (1978). They interviewed
over 400 women living in Camberwell in London in
1969 and 1974 and found that between 20 and 40 per
cent of their sample had some psychological problems
during the previous year which approached clinical
severity. Of these the great majority turned out to be
cases of depression, often associated with some severe
stress usually revolving around the loss of an important
person by separation or death. However, as is to be
expected, there were a number of other women in the
sample who had experienced a serious stressful episode in the same period of time but who did not
become depressed. Brown and Harris empirically
identified four factors in a woman's life which made
her vulnerable to the effects of stress and therefore
liable to become depressed. One of these factors was
not having paid employment outside the home (the
other three factors were: not having an intimate relationship with the husband or boy-friend, having three
or more children under 14 years of age living at home,
and early loss of mother). Although in this study paid
employment was not as potent a protector against the
effects of stress as having an intimate and confiding
relationship with someone else, in the absence of such
a relationship having a job almost halved the number
of women who became depressed following a severe
life event.

Cochrane and Stopes-Roe (1981c), in a community
survey in England, found that having paid employment
also reduced the number of symptoms of depression
reported by married women – although it is interesting
to note that paid employment did not significantly
affect other symptoms of psychological distress. Just

as important as far as the women in this survey were concerned was whether or not their husband was employed. Women with husbands out of work not only tended to be more depressed than women with husbands in work but they were also considerably more anxious. Indeed, having an unemployed husband seemed to be a more important factor in producing psychological symptoms than whether or not the woman herself was at work.

In the United States Radloff (1975) not only looked for an interaction between sex, marital status and employment among women in causing depression but she also asked her respondents about the importance of their job to them. She found that working married women were less depressed than non-working married women but were still more depressed than working men. However, she also found that the women in her survey reported equal degrees of job satisfaction as did the men. In other words, Gove's speculation about women's employment being relatively less satisfying psychologically was not borne out. One further point in all this merits attention: both Cochrane and Stopes-Roe (1980a) and Radloff (in the study just referred to) found that the unemployed *men* in their sample also experienced very high rates of psychological symptoms. Therefore having a job contributes not only to the psychological wellbeing of women but is equally important for both sexes.

Rosenfield (1980) took these analyses to their logical conclusion by looking at the reciprocal effects of employment of one spouse on the psychological status of the other. She found that women had more symptoms of depression in families where the husband was working but the wife was at home. The position was reversed in families where both spouses worked – men had more depressive symptoms than women. This reversal was caused both by the lower depression scores of working wives compared to housewives but in part also by the higher levels of depression of husbands with working wives. It is quite possible that the psychological advantages to a woman of being at work may have some adverse consequences for her husband. Presumably this is because he loses the status of sole breadwinner and also some of the home comforts provided by having a wife who does not work. In our study in England (Cochrane and Stopes-Roe 1980a), however, we did not find this pattern. Although husbands' employment status had direct and immediate consequences for the psychological wellbeing of their wives, the reverse was not true. In Britain it appears that whether or not a woman is at work has no significant impact on the psychological wellbeing of her husband.

A study by Hornung and McCullough (1981) in the USA looked at the effect of the relative educational and occupational statuses achieved by husbands and wives on the partner's happiness with their marriage. In the situation where the wife has higher occupational and/or educational prestige than her husband, although she was found to be satisfied with her marriage, he was likely to report marital dissatisfaction. This reversal of the traditional sex hierarchy of achievement which puts the husband in a somewhat inferior position was found uncomfortable by men. The opposite was true for women. 'Men find marriage to an "overeducated" woman stressful, while achievement-oriented women find marriage to an "overeducated" husband to be satisfying.' (Hornung and McCullough 1981: 138) In Britain in the 1980s the situation in the vast majority of dual employment marriages is such that the husband's occupational prestige is higher than the wife's so the kind of stress predicted by the study of status incompatibilities is relatively unlikely to arise. Hopefully as sex equality in education and occupation is approached there will be a corresponding diminution of sex role stereotypes that will make all varieties of relative status patterns in marriage equally tolerable.

All these findings taken together quite seriously undermine Gove's explanation of sex differences based upon the constricted role of the housewife to which most women are supposedly confined.

Before attempting to reach any conclusions it is perhaps important to introduce a note of caution here. The association between having paid employment outside the home and psychological wellbeing (and indeed the relationship between marital status and psychological disorder itself) has been assumed to be a cause-and-effect relationship. There is, however, the possibility that people with psychological problems are less likely to find or keep steady employment than those without these problems – it may even be that psychologically unstable individuals are selected out of the marriage market, either by never finding a partner or by becoming divorced or separated should they once marry. More likely than either of these simple cause-and-effect hypotheses is a more complex interactive process whereby depression and marital status are dependent and independent variables at the same time. Indeed, a complete explication of the relationship will have to take account of a variety of other status variables such as social class position and ethnic group membership as well as those discussed here (Warr and Parry 1982).

Conclusions

Sex differences in rates of mental illness present perhaps one of the clearest examples of the social creation of mental illness. Given that any biological explanation of the observed differences is extremely unlikely then we are left with a choice between the explanations based upon the traditional roles society assigns to women to explain their higher rates of psychological disorder, or the particular role played by married women, or some combination of the two. Given the weight of evidence it seems likely that the traditional sex role definitions for women, which carry the implication that positive coping behaviour is unfeminine and make it more likely that women will be relatively socially isolated (especially those who do not have a career), may make women both more vulnerable to psychological disorder and less able to withstand emotional disturbance without seeking professional help than are men. Being married in itself may not offer the psychological advantages to women that it apparently does to men because if Brown's findings are to be relied upon then only just over 60 per cent of women in one particular working-class district of London had the kind of marital relationship that would offer these advantages (Brown and Harris 1978). A major difference between married men and married women is the probability of being in employment. Although many more women are at work now than previously there are still fewer women than men in employment and it is perhaps towards employment that we should be looking as one of the major determinants of sex differences in psychopathology.

Chapter 4

Environmental effects on mental health

In the late 1960s several factors converged to produce a strong feeling that the environment which we had created for ourselves was having strong ill-effects on our psychological wellbeing. First there was a growing concern about the size of the world population. Figures such as an increase of 215,000 to the world population every day were becoming well known, and fears that the rate of population increase was outstripping the world's natural resources also became widespread. Then there was a high level of concern, especially in the United States, but later in other areas as well, that large cities and especially the inner ring were producing a vast number of problems which were intractable to any possible remedy. Crimes of violence, mugging, drug addiction, alcoholism, prostitution and other symptoms of social decay were assumed to be common characteristics of the inner city.

At the same time several authors popularized what was then known as the science of ethology. Books such as Desmond Morris's *The Naked Ape*, Richard Ardrey's *The Territorial Imperative* and Lionel Tiger's *Men in Groups* sold by the million. The common theme of these books was that man's current social behaviour could only be fully understood by reference to atavistic impulses which had been with us throughout evolution. Contemporary behaviours were thought to be conditioned by a primitive environment and thus in many ways incompatible with the highly organized social environment which we now inhabit.

A precursor of this revival of interest had been the 'flight or fight' theory of emotional arousal which postulated that some illnesses, such as hypertension, could be precipitated by an automatic emotional response to frustration which, while it may have been appropriate to the jungle or savannah, was not capable of finding a genuine outlet in the more constrained environment of today's urban industrial society. Thus a chronic level of emotional arousal which was evolved to enhance the fighting or fleeing capability of the organism might be responsible for a range of physical and psychological disorders (see Chapter 6).

The final element to which reference must be made was the publication of the results of a series of remarkable experiments by an American psychologist, John B. Calhoun (1962). Calhoun used the laboratory Norway rat for his experiments. He placed a number of individuals in a room 4.2 by 3 metres and gave them access to unlimited quantities of food and water. He allowed the population to increase naturally until it reached about twice the number that he believed could occupy the available space without too much stress. He observed these 'overcrowded' colonies for up to sixteen months. The most spectacular change in the behaviour of the animals occurred in the area of 'behavioural pathology'. He found that many females were unable to carry pregnancy to full term, some died while they were giving birth and many more were unable to care adequately for their offspring. This meant that the infant mortality rate of the rats reached very high levels – 96 per cent in some of the experiments. The male animals, too, exhibited extreme behavioural disturbances which ranged from 'sexual deviation to cannibalism and from phrenetic overactivity to a pathological withdrawal from which individuals would emerge to eat, drink and move about only when other members of the community were asleep'. (Calhoun 1962: 139). The sexual deviation referred to in the quotation included homosexuality, hypersexuality, a complete lack of interest in sex on the part of some males and in others a breakdown of the normal courtship ritual which is characteristic of the species. In fact it was this breakdown of normal social patterns of interactions among the rats which most interested Calhoun. The increased density in population meant that the rats were encountering each other far more frequently in their daily life than they would in the wild state. Consequently many of them were unable to maintain normal territorial behaviour and normal dominance hierarchies. This led to far more fights, and possibly far more vicious fights, than would otherwise have occurred.

Calhoun suggested that his experiments may contribute to the eventual understanding of similar problems confronting human beings. It was not long, in fact, before sociologists began to try and extrapolate to humans from Calhoun's findings (and a number of other ethologists who had produced analogous results on other species – for example Christian, Flyger and Davies (1960) using deer; Clough (1965) with lemmings; and Sugiyama (1964) with wild monkeys). These inquiries led in several directions which will be explored in turn in the remainder of this chapter.

The urban environment

The factors already described, taken together with the well ingrained belief in our culture that urban living is in some sense unnatural, have led to the assumption that city dwellers experience greater levels of stress, and consequently greater levels of psychological disorder, than do country dwellers. The anti-urban bias in prevailing mythology has a long history both in Britain and in the United States. Srole (1972) traces this back at least as far as the Old Testament with its imprecations against Sodom and Gomorrah. The belief that large cities are centres of vice and corruption as well as having damaging influences on physical and mental health is itself largely an urban phenomenon. Urban-based intellectuals writing with nostalgia about the glories of the simple life in the countryside have not necessarily reflected the views of the inhabitants of rural areas who, for the last 200 years at least, have striven mightily to migrate to cities whenever possible.

Many of the early and still influential American sociologists subscribed to this romanticized image of the rural environment as being distinctly preferable to the urban environment in which they were constrained to live. This general feeling for a time remained the unquestioned wisdom within the social sciences – namely that the city was a source of stress for man who was biologically more suited to living in the country. Only recently has this bias begun to be corrected, notably by such people as Banfield (1970) and other writers who have pointed out the great advantages of the urban over the rural environment.

Gross statistical studies of rates of mental disorder as reflected by rates of admission to mental hospital which compare urban and rural areas have not proved very useful. In general, the older of these studies did tend to show that rates of mental illness in urban areas were higher than rates of similar illnesses in rural areas. However, these data have uniformly failed to control for differences in provision of facilities in the two kinds of environment. A major determinant of mental hospital admission rates, as is pointed out elsewhere in this book, is and always has been the availability of psychiatric beds. Srole (1972) quotes the use made of the fact that black slaves in the southern States had much lower rates of admission to mental hospital than did freed blacks who had left to live in the North. Those people who were impressed by this difference and drew suitable political conclusions from it had conveniently overlooked the fact that there were no mental hospital beds for blacks in the South.

Comparisons made more recently, when the level of provision of psychiatric facilities has been more nearly similar in urban and rural areas, have shown a much more ambiguous picture. In England rates of admission are available for each of the country's fourteen Regional Health Authorities (DHSS 1980). The areas covered by these authorities are inevitably large and quite heterogeneous – it is not really possible to identify purely urban or rural regions. However, some comparisons are possible. On the basis of the figures in Table 7 one can see that both admission to mental hospitals and the number of resident patients at any given time are highest in the Mersey, Yorkshire and Thames districts, in which the people live mainly in

Table 7   Rates of admission and residence in mental hospitals in England per 100,000 population in 1977 by area

Regional Health Authority area	Admissions	Resident patients
Northern	382	179
Yorkshire	424	196
Trent	335	152
East Anglia	335	154
Combined Thames*	408	207
Wessex	392	150
Oxford	271	99
South-Western	368	164
West Midlands	334	152
Mersey	436	235
North-Western	385	149
Average for England	378	176

Source: Adapted from DHSS 1980
* Average of the four Thames Health Authorities

large cities. Rates are low in Oxford and East Anglia – predominantly rural areas. However, the heavily urbanized areas of West Midlands and Trent also have *low* rates while the South-West has somewhat higher rates. Wessex has a relatively high rate for admission but a relatively low rate of residence in mental hospitals. These patterns are quite stable over the years and enable no firm conclusions to be drawn about the effects on mental health of urban versus rural living.

Dohrenwend and Dohrenwend (1974) report a re-analysis of nine community surveys which directly compared urban and rural rates of psychological disorder. Although seven of the nine studies found that the urban areas sampled had higher rates than did the rural areas, the differences observed were actually small, ranging from 0.08 per cent to 14 per cent. Equally it was found that the population of urban areas generally exhibited a higher level of neurosis and personality disorders but the more serious psychotic conditions, particularly depression, were more frequently found in rural areas. A consistent difference in the urban and rural rates of schizophrenia could not be determined from these studies.

When considering results such as these one must ask about the relationship between the independent variable which is measured – namely urban/rural residence – and the longer life experiences of the individuals concerned. This century has seen a continuation of the general drift away from rural areas to urban areas and it is only to be expected that a proportion of those found to be suffering from psychological disorders in an urban area will in fact have originated from a rural area. For example, in the Midtown Manhattan studies referred to elsewhere in this book the majority of those residents of Manhattan who had severe psychological problems had in fact originated from small towns or rural areas and subsequently moved into the inner city.

In fact, of course, in an area like Britain the differences in the rural and urban environment are relatively small when set against their underlying similarities. Only a very small proportion of the population live in a truly rural environment. Many more live in small to medium-sized towns surrounded by country but their life style is probably far more similar to the life style of people living in large metropolitan areas than it is to the life style of the truly rural inhabitant. The small size of the British Isles, the ease of communications and transport, the intrusion of a common media system and of an increasingly similar pattern of consumption in all areas, together with the standardization of wage rates and welfare benefits and so on, has meant that any differences that exist between the urban and rural environment are bound to be small compared to differences, say, between social class environments or between the social environments of the two sexes.

Finally, it should perhaps be pointed out that the difference in the physical health of urban and rural dwellers which has traditionally favoured those in rural areas has recently been reversed. On indices such as infant mortality and death from infectious diseases it now seems that the city dweller is in a superior position to the country dweller. This is presumably due to the somewhat higher standard of living in cities and the better provision of health care facilities in large urban areas. It is quite likely that the same trend that has influenced the physical differential has also influenced the mental health differential, if indeed it ever existed.

Crowding and mental health

The area which has seen the most attempts to draw a direct parallel between the animal studies of Calhoun and others and human populations has been that of population density and pathology. Several investigators have in fact looked for direct analogies of the behavioural pathology shown by Calhoun's rats and behavioural pathologies exhibited by human populations. Winsborough (1965) and Factor and Waldron (1973) each identified a series of indices of human behaviour which they believed directly paralleled pathological rat behaviour. Thus, for example, infant mortality rate in humans was equated with the infant mortality rate in rats, public assistance rate to children was equated with failure of rats to care for their offspring, and mental hospitalization was equated with the extreme social withdrawal exhibited by some animals. Sometimes crime rates have been taken as a measure of the aggressive tendency displayed by the overcrowded rats.

These early studies showed, as was to be expected, that there were correlations between the density of a dwelling area (often community areas of Chicago) and the various indices of social pathology. For example, Factor and Waldron found a strong correlation between mental hospital admission rates and areal density. Winsborough found moderately strong correlations between population density, infant mortality, public assistance to young people and tuberculosis rates. However, these findings cannot be taken at their face value. Both studies included a number of control variables in order to take account of other factors which were believed to be correlated with the density of the area in which people lived. Thus Winsborough found that when he partialled out statistically the effect of social class and some other variables, the relationship between density and the death rate was reversed – in other words a *lower* death rate was associated with *higher* density living conditions.

Factor and Waldron, too, present information which shows not only that mental hospital admissions correlate with density per square mile but also that they correlate with the proportion of the population who had recently moved. In fact this correlation is considerably stronger (0.74) than the original correlation between mental hospital admissions and density (0.63) thus supporting the idea that perhaps people with a predisposition to mental ill-health are more likely to move into the more densely populated areas of cities. They also report a negative correlation between likelihood of mental hospital admission and percentage of the population who own their own houses (which may be taken as a good measure of social class). Areas with a large proportion of owner occupiers tend to be areas of low density and tend to have low mental hospital admission rates.

Subsequent work has shown that these early attempts to apply the models developed by Calhoun and others to human populations were both premature and poorly executed. Freedman (1979) has pointed out that there was a tendency for social scientists as well as the general public to be overly impressed with the studies of Calhoun at the expense of methodologically sounder studies which produced much more ambiguous results. Freedman cites a series of studies which produced some results analagous to those found by Calhoun but which showed that the behavioural phenomena exhibited by the animals were in fact unrelated to density. Thus, in one study on rats the pattern of interference with successful reproduction was observed. In one group this happened when a population of sixteen was reached, while in identical physical conditions another colony reached a population of over 100 before this phenomenon exhibited itself. Even when these animals were suddenly given double the amount of space they had previously enjoyed there was no sign that their population rose to fill that space. It seems that the limiting factor was the psychological property of being enclosed in a physical space rather than the actual density of population. This obviously has important implications for studies on humans where cognitive control of behaviour and cognitive interpretations of the environment are likely to be even more salient factors than they are in non-human populations.

More seriously still has been the naivety of some of the attempts to apply animal models to human populations. We only have to look at the attempts to measure the variables involved to see that some of these studies were bound to produce misleading results. If we take the independent variable – density – first. Areal density, that is number of people per square kilometre, is unlikely to be a very important aspect of crowding in humans. The attraction of this variable is that it is easy to measure in aggregate studies of the relationship between density and mental illness based upon city wards or census tracts. The disadvantage lies in the fact that it is not directly related to the day-to-day experience of the individuals living in the relatively crowded or uncrowded area. If an area has many high-rise developments, for example, its population per hectare is likely to be high. This does not necessarily mean, however, that each individual has a smaller space in which to live.

The extent to which a particular person will subjectively experience crowding is more likely to depend upon the size of dwelling he has and with how many people it is shared. This realization led to the measure 'persons per room' replacing areal density as the independent variable in ecological studies of crowding in humans. Even this definition of crowding has two serious weaknesses which reduce its psychological importance.

First there is the problem of the single person living alone in a one-room flat or bedsitter. Such accommodation is known to be associated with a very high risk of mental illness, either because of the social isolation often engendered by living alone or because vulnerable people seek this kind of accommodation.

However, as in most studies the average number of persons per room is *less* than 1, the person living alone in one room will appear statistically to be living in crowded conditions! Because the definition used puts the most vulnerable group toward the overcrowded end of the dimension it artificially inflates any apparent relationship between density and pathology. It is patently nonsense to suggest that the psychological vulnerability of someone living alone is due to overcrowding.

The second difficulty with the 'persons per room' measure is the impact that children have upon it. For most families the main determinant of density is the number of children they have. Now it may be that in extreme cases the presence of children causes problems purely because of a lack of space but in most cases any negative effect on mental health is more likely to be mediated by other intervening variables such as the mother being unable to work or becoming effectively confined to the home – whatever its size. Remember, too, that it is only very recently that having children has become defined as a factor in the aetiology of psychological disturbance – previously children were thought of as a blessing, particularly for their mother.

Consider one of the better designed studies which has looked for associations between crowding and psychological disorder. Using five indices of social pathology (standardized mortality ratio, fertility rate, public assistance for young people, delinquency rate and mental hospital admission rate) Galle, Gove and McPherson (1972) looked for correlations between these indices and density and various aspects of crowding. Initially they found that population density correlated positively with pathology. They proceeded to break down areal density into four indices of crowding, viz. persons per room, rooms per housing unit, housing unit per structure, and housing structures per acre. A combination of these four components of density evinced a very strong correlation with each of the indices of social pathology which was not eradicated by controlling for social class and ethnicity.

However, the correlation found between crowding and mental hospital admission rate (0.58) was undoubtedly influenced by the very much higher correlation (0.72) found between mental hospital admission rates and proportion of people in an area living alone. In fact, rooms per housing unit was the best predictor of mental hospital admission rates in their study. Now rooms per housing unit can also be taken as a measure of the number of people living on their own. Housing units with only one room tend to be bedsitters with single occupants. Housing units with more than one room are more likely to be family homes and thus this measure may be yet another indicator of the high levels of pathology found among those who are living in isolation.

Before leaving ecological level studies it is necessary to refer once again to the danger of the so-called ecological fallacy. In this context the danger is in assuming that because a person resides in a high-density area of a city (however defined) he himself will be in a crowded position. In even the most densely populated areas there will be some spacious homes, equally in the well-spaced suburbs one may find some families living in overcrowded conditions. For crowding to be taken as a variable which is causal of psychological problems it must be shown to have an influence on individuals as well as on an aggregate level.

With these strictures in mind it is worth turning to the results of those survey studies of the effects of crowding on mental wellbeing which actually investigated the effects on individuals of various degrees of crowding.

A large-scale study of housing variables and a variety of reactions to them has been carried out in

Toronto by Booth and others (Booth 1976; Booth and Cowell 1976; Booth and Edwards 1976). Working-class families living in high and low density areas of the city were interviewed and asked to undergo a thorough medical examination. They were also asked about the extent to which they felt themselves to be crowded. None of the crowding variables (areal density, household density, subjective crowding) were consistently related to mental or physical health. More crowded households did report more quarrels and more feelings of dissatisfaction with life but even these differences were small. Booth himself was apparently quite surprised that crowding had such miniscule detectable effects on the health and wellbeing of his respondents (Booth 1976).

In what is perhaps the definitive study to date, Gove, Hughes and Galle (1979) obtained results which contradicted those of Booth. They interviewed over 2,000 residents of the various census districts of Chicago selected in such a way as to minimize the potential confounding of crowding with low income. They achieved this by taking their sample from districts which were (a) poor and crowded, (b) poor and uncrowded, (c) well-off and crowded, (d) well-off and uncrowded. The authors also controlled the racial composition of the areas they sampled in the same way.

Apart from the usual objective definition of crowding (persons per room) they developed indices of subjective experience of, and reactions to, crowding. The indices were made up of questions designed to measure *lack of privacy* (e.g. 'At home does it seem as if you can never be by yourself?') and *overload of social demands* (e.g. 'At home does it seem as if you almost never have any peace and quiet?'). Although actual household density was correlated with the subjective feelings of being crowded it was by no means the only predictor – for example, at the same household density women reported more social demands and less privacy than did men.

Gove *et al.* measured various aspects of mental health such as number of psychological symptoms, extent of positive emotional experiences, feelings of being on the verge of a nervous breakdown and irritability, as well as physical health, social relationships in the home and quality of child care. Household density was definitely related to poorer mental health (and the other social variables) but this relationship was mediated by the psychological experiences of lack of privacy and being met with constant demands from others at home. People who reported this subjective experience of crowding (whatever their objective situation) also reported feeling 'washed out' and tired much of the time, being unable to make plans for the future, having a strong desire to get away from it all and attempting to withdraw psychologically from the unwanted presence of others by not listening to them or ignoring their requests.

Gove *et al.'s* study makes a distinct theoretical advance on previous survey work on overcrowding because it illuminates the psychological processes which intervene between actual crowding and mental strain. There are, however, one or two points of weakness with the study which cannot be ignored. First, only just over half of those who were approached agreed to be interviewed and such a high non-response rate inevitably raises the possibility of biased sampling. Second, people living alone (22%) were excluded from the analysis because they were unable to report on the subjective experiences of crowding. The high rate of mental illness of the 'crowded' isolate has already been commented upon. The authors also suggest that they found a 'strong' relationship between objective and subjective crowding and poor mental health. In the sense that the crowding variables were better predictors of psychological disturbance than the other independent variables included in the study (sex, age, education, income, race, marital status) this claim is true. In an absolute sense, however, household crowding, both objective and subjective, is only a weak predictor of psychological status. In fact less than 5 per cent of the variability in psychological wellbeing was accounted for by the combined objective and subjective measure of crowding.

Finally, it is worth returning to an earlier study of the effects of crowding because of the much higher levels of density with which it dealt. Mitchell (1971) carried out three surveys in Hong Kong involving a total of over 7,000 people, including nearly 600 husband-wife pairs. The living density levels which he recorded, and which may be regarded as normative in Hong Kong, would be regarded as almost intolerable elsewhere in the world. The average living area per person was only 4 square metres. Twenty-eight per cent of respondents slept three or more to a bed and almost 40 per cent shared their dwellings with non-kinsmen.

Shortage of living space was reported as unpleasant by respondents but had little effect on mental health and what effects Mitchell did find were confined to the poorer members of the community. Higher densities did produce more stresses and strains in parent-child relationships and on relationships with other people outside the home but not on husband-wife relationships. Significantly, having to share a dwelling with non-relatives produced more mental health problems than crowding *per se*.

It is obvious that there is no simple relationship between crowding and mental health and perhaps we have not yet succeeded in getting at the crucial psychological dimensions of any relationship which does exist.

Freedman (1975) has provided a valuable perspective on the effects of crowding on human behaviour in general and, although he arrived at his model of crowding after a series of laboratory experimental studies, his approach may have relevance for mental health. On the basis of his own experiments and the researches of others Freedman concluded that

> high density does not have a generally negative effect on humans. Neither long-term exposure to vast numbers of people in small spaces (cities), nor lives spent in cramped and crowded dwellings . . . causes people to respond negatively . . . Our second conclusion concerning the effects of crowding upon humans is that high density makes other people a more important stimulus and thereby intensifies the typical reaction to them . . . whatever the interpersonal situation, higher density will cause the individual's reaction to be stronger. (Freedman 1975: 104–5)

Extrapolating Freedman's conclusions to the relationship between crowding and mental health leads to a hypothesis that those who are for some *other* reason susceptible to psychological disturbance will be even more vulnerable if they live in overcrowded conditions. Those who are psychologically more robust will experience no negative consequences of crowding and indeed may relish the intensity of social contact it provides and feel deprived and lonely if they are isolated. In any event, crowding does not appear to be sufficient on its own to produce psychological problems.

Housing conditions

Other aspects of housing apart from density have also been suspected of being capable of causing mental ill health. Again this is an area where myths and fashions in beliefs have outstripped the empirical evidence. Nevertheless, significant changes in housing policies have occurred because of the assumed effects of housing type upon people's wellbeing. The most remarkable of these changes of direction has been the decision to build, or not to build, high-rise flats. Increasingly, too, the suspicion has grown that large new housing estates, particularly council housing estates, whether or not they are designed on the high-rise principle, are to some extent incompatible with social and personal welfare. These two aspects of the housing environment will be dealt with separately.

In 1968, 20 per cent of all planned new local authority housing in England was scheduled as high rise (i.e. buildings with 6 or more storeys); five years later, in 1973, this proportion had fallen to 2 per cent (McGinty 1974). Meanwhile more than one million people had been housed in high rise blocks of flats. Several factors produced this change of mind among urban planners, including the publicity given to the high cost of maintenance of these buildings and the fact that some towers had collapsed! However, it is probably true to say that most important of all was the belief that high-rise accomodation had been responsible for numerous social and individual psychological problems. This is not the place to review studies of vandalism and crime in different types of housing schemes but an inspection of the studies of psychological disorder and floor level reveals surprisingly little evidence of the pathogenic qualities of high-rise buildings. The issue is obviously complicated by the possibility of self-selection and type of accommodation. No one has ever suggested that living in a penthouse suite high above the Thames or in a luxury apartment in a tower block on Lakeshore Drive in Chicago has adverse effects on mental health. The research has basically concerned itself with people in lower quality public housing who often have little choice of accommodation and who may be relatively recent arrivals in a very new environment.

In the study by Mitchell to which reference has already been made it was noted that floor level had no effect on mental health overall. It did interact with having to share accommodation with non-kinsmen such that those living on upper storeys had more symptoms. A major effect that was noticed, however, was the difficulty parents in higher flats had in supervising children playing outside and the anxiety for their safety this brought.

Fanning (1967) produced similar results from his survey of 1,100 wives of British servicemen in Germany. The women who were assigned living accommodation in flats had more illnesses, including the psychoneuroses, than those assigned to houses and there was a similar relationship between floor level and neuroses. Women who lived on the higher levels not only had more neurotic symptoms but also reported more loneliness than those on ground levels, a finding confirmed by Gilloran (1968). Because of the difficulties of supervision the women in flats may have been more likely to insist that children play inside and have become tense because of this. The flats in Fanning's study were no higher than 4 storeys so may not produce conditions comparable to those in blocks of 16 or 20 storeys.

Richman (1974) did in fact look at the rates of psychiatric problems among mothers of young children in high-rise tower blocks compared to another sample in low-rise flats and a third sample in ordinary houses. He, however, observed no substantial difference in the occurrence of problems in the three groups.

Where then does the assumption that high level living can cause psychological problems come from? Well, several less than systematic studies by general practitioners and other doctors (e.g. Hird 1967; Gilloran 1968; both cited in Martin *et al.* 1976) strongly suggested that there were both physical and mental health costs associated with living high up in tower blocks. This has only been confirmed, and then only partly, by two well designed and controlled studies.

Ineichen and Hooper (1974) interviewed about 250 families living in various kinds of new housing in Bristol including detached suburban houses, new terraced houses in the inner city, maisonettes and high-rise flats on an inner-city redevelopment. For inclusion in the study the parents had to live together and have at least one child at home. The families were interviewed after they had been living in the new environment for approximately eighteen months. A very simple index of what the authors call 'mental illness' was used which involved asking respondents if they had experienced headaches, sleeplessness, nerves and undue depression in the past month. Those who reported the symptoms were called neurotic. Using this crude classification scheme it was found that those living in high-rise flats had a greater proportion of neurotics than those living in most other types of housing, although all the redeveloped inner-city areas had more than their share of problems.

A follow-up study conducted eighteen months later (Hooper and Ineichen 1979) involved reinterviewing those families still living in the same accommodation. There was strong evidence that an 'adjustment effect' had occurred. The overall rate of neuroses diminished significantly between the two studies and the difference between the types of housing was also reduced such that those in the high-rise flats were indistinguishable from those in other types of housing. However, 60 per cent of the high-rise families moved out between the interviews (a period of only eighteen months on average) and there was a strong suspicion that poor mental health at the initial interview was associated with likelihood of moving away.

These findings neatly illustrate the methodological problems surrounding studies in this area. There may very well be a complex interaction between psychological status, morbidity and family status as well as other demographic and personal variables and type of accommodation sought. The final and most important study of the psychological effects of high-rise housing also encountered problems of this kind.

Gillis (1977) interviewed 442 public housing residents in Calgary and Edmonton, Canada, including some who lived on the sixteenth floor of high-rise apartment blocks. Psychological distress was measured by a scale of fifteen symptoms very similar in format and content to the Langner 22-Item Index (see Appendix 1). In the total sample there was no apparent correlation between floor level and psychological symptoms but further analysis revealed that there was in fact an interaction with sex. Floor level in flats was a strong and direct predictor of psychological distress among women but the relationship, although weaker, was in the opposite direction for men – the higher up they lived the better their mental health. Strangely, women living on the ground floor also exhibited higher levels of the mild neurotic symptoms measured. The correlation between floor level and symptoms only operated from floors 1 to 16. Several women expressed a feeling of vulnerability in living on the ground floor of a multi-floor block especially if there was no one else sharing the ground floor. In fact women in high-rise flats who shared a floor tended to have lower symptom levels than those who were the only residents on a particular floor. It seems that the loneliness and isolation which can engulf women in high-rise flats is much less likely to affect their husbands who are probably at work in the daytime and who may get enjoyment and stimulation from living high above the ground for only part of their day. Equally it should be remembered that Gillis only included families with a child under 12 years of age so that all the women had a motherly role (although some were working as well). It may very well be that childless women or women whose children have left home may enjoy high-rise living as much as do men.

Turning to the research that has been done on the psychological consequences of living on a new housing estate, an equally ambiguous picture emerges. On the one hand there is the strong feeling or suspicion of many people that the effects of being uprooted from previous well-established communities, even though delapidated, and rehoused in what are conceived of as barren housing estates designed without a thought for community life, would be isolation, withdrawal, loneliness and hence depression, particularly for non-working women. On the other hand when systematic attempts have been made to measure these ill-effects the results have been less than spectacular.

Perhaps a climate of opinion antipathetic to new housing estates existed which only required the hint of evidence in order for it to become confirmed as conventional wisdom. Such evidence was provided by one of the pioneering studies in this area conducted by Martin, F. M. *et al.* (1957). They very carefully documented all kinds of contact with psychiatric agencies (inpatient, outpatient and GP consultations) and the self-reported psychiatric symptoms of a subsample of people rehoused on a London County Council estate in Hertfordshire. The population of the village had grown from 5,000 in 1949 to 17,500 by 1954 because of rehousing. The results of this study are usually cited as supporting the notion that rehousing can bring psychological problems (e.g. in Martin, A. E. *et al.* 1976). True enough, the number of people from the estate receiving psychiatric treatment in 1954 was very high compared to the national average but two other aspects of the comparison are often ignored. First, the rate of psychological problems in the village was always very high even before the influx of new residents. The authors themselves quote ratios of estate to national average admission rates of 1.74:1 for 1949, and 1.72:1 for 1954. Although the treatment rate did go up on the estate by about 20 per cent during the period of expansion, it also went up by a similar amount elsewhere. Secondly, a comparison with a global national average is probably not very useful because of the variety of other factors apart from housing which may affect rates, such as the age, sex and social class structure of the population. It seems that the only conclusion that can be drawn from this particular study is that certain groups, for example middle-aged women, sometimes do react badly to rehousing and become neurotically depressed. However, even this tendency seems to ameliorate with time – women who had been on the estate longest had fewer symptoms.

Against this study must be set the results of three other major British studies and at least one from the USA. The results of these are so similar to each other that only the outlines need be given. Clout (1962) in Crawley New Town, Hare and Shaw (1965) in Croydon and Taylor and Chave (1964) in London all compared the mental health of residents of one or more types of new housing estate with the mental health of the residents of the kinds of areas the mover group had left behind. In each case the authors failed to find any substantial adverse effects whatsoever of the relocation. Taylor and Chave did find higher GP consultation rates for neurotic disorders in the New Town they studied but this occurred in spite of the fact that the prevalence of neurotic symptoms in the communities compared did not differ. It seemed that in the new environment people were less inhibited about asking their GP for help with psychological problems than were the remaining residents of the decaying London borough from which they came.

Finally Wilner *et al.* (1962) compared the mental and physical health of 300 black families rehoused from a city slum to a new housing development with that of 300 families who remained behind in the slums over a period of three years. On most measures and especially on the mental health measures the rehoused group showed an improvement during the three years after they were rehoused while the stationary group showed no such improvement.

How is it then that in these areas (urban-rural comparisons, the question of density, high-rise flats and new housing estates) the belief has grown up that psychological problems are produced and, indeed, how is it that these beliefs remain relatively unaffected by the empirical evidence? As was pointed out, it seems that for a variety of reasons the time was ripe for an idea like this to take hold. There exists just about enough evidence to feed the prejudices that came from other sources against certain types of environment and such beliefs are incredibly resilient. It has proved to be a very tempting simplification of reality to blame the increase in the use of mental health services that has undoubtedly occurred in the last several decades on the physical environment. Among other factors there have been vast shifts in the attitudes of people to their own mental health and that of others such that the expectations of, and tolerance levels for, distress have changed considerably. These changes, taken together with changes in family structure, sex role definitions and the availability of treatment, far outweigh the impact of residential effects except in extreme circumstances or where vulnerability already exists.

Chapter 5

Migration, culture and mental health

It is almost a truism to say that culture has a great influence on mental illness. By definition culture is one of the largest determinants of all behaviour, normal as well as abnormal, therefore, to the extent that we find different cultural patterns of normal behaviour, we should expect to find culturally determined differences in abnormal behaviour. It is not hard to discern the elements of social organization which may affect mental health, producing different types and rates of disorder in different cultures. Variations in the nature of religious beliefs, with more or less sexual and other libidinal restrictions and differential emphasis on guilt, is a salient feature of cultural divergence and is often considered to be a contributory factor in mental illness. Family structure and organization, too, with the complex of obligations, intense emotional involvements and the propensity for conflict and loss as well as support, shows a remarkable variability between cultures. The roles and statuses assigned to each sex, the relationships between parents and children, the emphasis placed on achievement, the traditions of drinking, historical relationships with other ethnic groups and the extent to which personal identity is bound up with cultural group membership, are but a few of the other ways in which culture may influence psychological vulnerability.

The medical model of mental illness, and the term 'mental illness' itself, has perhaps served to obscure this fact. Because many physical diseases such as tuberculosis, cancer and pneumonia find similar expression (although perhaps different incidence) in different cultures, this has led to the assumption that mental disease will also show a consistent pattern across cultures. This is but one of the unfortunate consequences of the reification of the disease concept in Western psychiatry.

At first sight it should be relatively easy to determine if there is universal agreement on what constitutes insanity in different cultures. This in fact does not turn out to be so easy, for several reasons. Perhaps the major problem is the fact that psychiatry itself is very much a Western discipline. Even in non-Western cultures psychiatrists usually have a Western type of training and therefore a Western nosology of psychiatric concepts. To some extent psychiatrists are bound to be influenced by their training when they are perceiving and interpreting various kinds of behaviours as symptoms of some underlying disorder. Thus, for example, Kapur *et al* (1974) in India found a similar range of symptoms in a community survey of a rural village as has been found in Great Britain and in the United States. Much of the debate about the cultural content of mental disorders has come down to a discussion of whether there are differences in rates of specific disorders rather than whether the same disorders actually exist.

The evidence from anthropological studies is perhaps most directly relevant here. Indeed, it was from the work of anthropologists that the idea of the cultural determinants of the definitions of normal and abnormal were first made apparent. Subsequently some anthropological investigations have looked to see whether the behaviour we regard as symptomatic of mental illness exists in other cultures and, if it does, to see whether it is also recognized there as indicating psychopathology. We can take as examples the three major categories in the Western psychiatric diagnostic scheme: depression, neuroses and schizophrenia. Depression in one form or another is probably the most common mental illness found in Britain and yet appears hardly to exist in some non-Western cultures. Not only is the concept not available in various languages such as Chinese, Japanese, Malay, and North American Indian languages, but the very symptoms that we regard as indicative of depression (feelings of hopelessness, irrational guilt, worthlessness and apathy) do not appear to exist in some other cultures (Marsella 1979).

Behaviours that we take to be symptomatic of neuroses do appear to exist or have equivalents in other cultural milieux, but in many cases there is no concept of neurosis as such. The behaviours may be recognized as odd or deviant but there is no attempt to infer any underlying illness process. Similarly, the behaviours are not linked together in a syndrome as Western psychiatry prefers. Thus, to a Western eye behaviours may very well exist in other cultures which would be recognizably the product of neuroses (anxiety, restlessness, compulsions and psychosomatic symptoms, etc.), but to local observers they are just seen as perhaps unusual but unrelated behaviour patterns.

Schizophrenia is perhaps the only concept which seems to have an almost universal acceptance. In many cultures and indeed in many historical periods, extreme social and emotional withdrawal, auditory hallucinations, delusions and flatness of emotional response have been taken to be indicative of some serious psychological disturbance (Murphy *et al.* 1963), although it has not always carried the stigma associated with the concept of schizophrenia in the West. Equally it appears that there is a relatively uniform rate of schizophrenia across different cultures – sometimes estimated at between 0.5 per cent to 1 per cent of the adult population. Even with schizophrenia, however, there appear to be very strong cultural determinants of prognosis and outcome. Murphy and Raman (1971), for example, found that although Great Britain and Mauritius had very similar incidence rates for schizophrenia, the prognosis for Mauritian patients was far better than for those in Britain. Although treatment in Mauritius was probably behind treatment in Britain in terms of availability of new drugs, Mauritian schizophrenics were far less likely to relapse and be readmitted to hospital than were British schizophrenics. This was attributed to the fact that the concept of schizophrenia in Britain implies a lifelong disability with periods of remission whereas in Mauritius the concept is much more equivalent to that we have for a physical infection, i.e. one has the disorder then is cured. Indeed, it has been found that generally prognosis is far better in Third World countries than in the West (World Health Organisation 1979).

When we come to consider the situation within a particular society, although there is some standardization of material and social environment produced by geographical proximity, there are other difficulties which emerge in the study of subcultural influences on mental health. The study of cultural influences in Britain, for example, is confounded with migration. Most of the major subcultures currently to be found in this country were brought here by immigrants. There are as yet relatively few adults who are ethnically West Indian, Indian or Pakistani who were born in this country. Thus when we look for differences in mental health across different subcultural groups we have to take into account the fact that many of the individual members of those groups experienced the possible traumas of migration as well as belonging to cultural minorities.

Before turning to an examination of the largest cultural minorities in Britain one by one, it is perhaps worthwhile to look at differences in rates of mental illness that exist within two areas of Britain with only slightly divergent cultures: England and Scotland. The rates of admission to mental hospital in Scotland are much higher than are the rates in England, and Scots living in England have a still higher rate than native-born Scots in Scotland. The largest part of these differentials is accounted for by alcohol-related disorders. For example, English men are admitted to mental hospital with alcoholism at the rate at about 28 per 100,000 population per year, while in Scotland the equivalent rate is 158 per 100,000 (Cochrane 1980b). Scots in England have a rate 50 per cent higher again. Although no study exists which has directly accounted for this difference in the rate of alcoholism, it is highly probable that historically established cultural differences in drinking patterns north and south of the border put Scots at a far greater risk of alcoholism than the English.

When such slight differences in culture as those that exist between England and Scotland produce such tremendous variations in one form of psychological disorder, it might be expected that the much larger cultural differences which exist between the English and say the Pakistani-born residents of this country would produce even larger variations in psychological status. Indeed, in a booklet published by the Community Relations Commission (1976) with the title *Aspects of mental health in a multicultural society*, the view was clearly expressed that the minority ethnic groups in Britain were at much higher risk of mental illness than were natives. Groups who were considered as being especially high risk included Moslem women,

Hindu women, Sikh women, West Indian women, Asian men, West Indian men and elderly immigrants!

There is a very strong background assumption that immigrants will have poorer mental (and incidentally physical) health than will the native populations they join. At first glance this assumption seems to be well founded. A very early study in this area (Ødegaard 1932) suggested that some forms of psychological disorder, especially schizophrenia, predisposed people to become migrants. There are two other major reasons why immigrants may have higher rates of mental illness than natives as well as the selective migration hypothesis.

It is undoubtedly true that for many individuals international migration is a stress-producing experience. Even if the actual journey is relatively uneventful family ties are often temporarily broken and international migration usually assumes a concomitant rural to urban transition. This implies finding a new and different job and adapting to a totally different life style. One can hardly imagine a much greater change of environment than would be experienced by a person who one day was a farmer in the Punjab and the next found himself working in a factory or foundry in Wolverhampton. It has often been observed, too, that many immigrants have unrealistic expectations of the society they are joining and that there is the likelihood of frustrations when these expectations are not met.

There is another cluster of problems arising from immigrant/host interaction. The most obvious of these is the prejudice likely to be experienced by the immigrant arising from the hostility of the host community. Prejudice has been a marked feature of British life in the past decade, and is an added difficulty with which immigrants have to cope. In most cases, too, immigrants enter the lowest economic stratum in the host society. They typically take the jobs that native workers are no longer content to fill either because they are unpleasant or underpaid or both. We have already observed that low social class is associated with high rates of psychological disorder, therefore it may be expected that if immigrants are disproportionately represented in the lowest social class then they will experience correspondingly higher rates of disorder. As with jobs, accommodation tends to be a serious problem for immigrants. They find that they are only able to afford accommodation in those areas of the cities which the white native population is ready to vacate because they are disintegrating. Paradoxically this may occasionally work to the psychological benefit of the immigrant groups as the concentration of new arrivals in certain well defined areas may work to reduce the possibility of social isolation which in turn is one of the factors likely to be related to depression and psychological breakdown.

Migration and mental health

Possibly the earliest study of the mental illness rates of immigrants was published by the United States Census Bureau in 1906. In a census of all state mental hospitals on 31 December 1903 the Bureau found that foreign-born residents of the United States constituted 30 per cent of all patients compared to only 20 per cent of the non-hospital population. When this study was repeated in 1910 the Bureau again found that the foreign-born were grossly overrepresented in the mental hospitals compared to their numbers in the population. The general conclusion from these two surveys was that Europe was dumping genetic degenerates in the United States and that there should be some tightening-up of immigration laws. This recommendation was implemented and health screening for immigrants at Ellis Island in New York began to include checks on psychological status. What the Bureau failed to appreciate at that time was that there were numerous and and substantial demographic differences between the foreign-born and the native-born in the United States. The foreign-born tended to be younger, male, single, tended to live in urban areas and were heavily concentrated in the lower social class groups. All of these factors are in themselves related to a higher probability of mental illness. It was only much later that a series of studies by Malzberg (e.g. Malzberg 1962; 1964; 1968; 1969; Malzberg and Lee 1956) applied the appropriate controls to the figures and obtained a more realistic comparison. In his study of admissions to mental hospitals in New York State between 1929 and 1931, for example, he found that, given their numbers in the state as a whole, the foreign-born were overrepresented by 91 per cent in mental hospitals. When, however, the figures were standardized for age and sex, the excess dropped to 19 per cent and when he added further controls for urban/rural residence the excess almost entirely disappeared. He was also to observe that the country of origin of immigrants was a significant factor. Thus, for example, immigrants to the United States from England had a rate of mental illness *lower* than that of native-born Americans, lower in fact than the American-born offspring of parents from England. A similar pattern has been observed by Murphy (1977) in Canada, and Krupinski and Stoller (1965) in Australia.

Recently there has been an upsurge of interest in the psychological health of immigrants to Britain stimulated by this research in other countries and by the increasing (although still small by comparison with the USA) proportion of the British population composed of immigrants and their descendants. This interest has usually been accompanied by the assumption that ethnic minorities in Britain, and immigrants in particular, pay a psychological price for their adaptation to a British way of life (Commission for Racial Equality 1978;

Table 8   Mental hospital admission rates of natives and immigrants in Britain, 1971

(a) *Crude rates per 100,000 population*	
Natives	265
Immigrants	495

(b) *Age-sex standardized rates per 100,000 adults*	
Native	494
Irish	1110
Indian	403
Pakistani	336
West Indian	539

Source: Adapted from Cochrane and Stopes-Roe 1981b

Littlewood and Lipsedge 1982: 125–52). There were several studies in the 1960s which compared the mental hospital admission rate of natives and immigrants (for example Hemsi 1967; Hashmi 1968; Bagley 1972; and Hitch 1976), all of which reported finding higher rates of mental illness among the immigrants. However, these studies had some of the same weaknesses as the original United States Census Bureau survey – they failed to standardize for known demographic differences between the native-born and immigrants. Some of these errors were compounded by the fact that only a very small base population was studied, usually the patients admitted to a single mental hospital. Cochrane (1977) carried out the first national survey of mental hospital statistics for immigrants in Britain. The unstandardized figures showed a clear excess of immigrants over native admissions: compared to their numbers in the population, immigrants were almost twice as likely to be admitted to a mental hospital than were natives (see Table 8). However, when the 146,000 mental hospital admissions in 1971 were analysed more carefully and appropriate controls on the data applied, the picture changed dramatically. Of the numerically largest immigrant groups in this country, only the Irish-born and to a much lesser extent the West Indian-born communities contributed more than their share of mental patients compared to natives. As is shown in Table 8, people born in India and Pakistan had conspicuously lower rates of admission to mental hospital than did the English-born.

It is immediately apparent that the likelihood of being admitted to mental hospital is not directly related to the probable difficulties encountered by the immigrant in adjusting to a new life in this country. Those with relatively few transitions to make (e.g. the Irish) seemed to be much more vulnerable than those with many transitions to make (e.g. the Asian groups). A more detailed analysis of these figures broken down by diagnosis showed that the high rate for those born in the Republic of Ireland, like the Scots referred to earlier, was in large part accounted for by alcohol-related disorders, although they also had considerably higher rates of schizophrenia than did the English (see Table 9).

Table 9   Sex specific rates of mental hospital admissions by selected diagnoses and country of birth per 100,000 population, 1971

Country of birth	All diagnoses		Alcohol related		Schizophrenia and related	
	Male	Female	Male	Female	Male	Female
England and Wales	434	551	28	8	87	87
Scotland	712	679	218	46	90	97
Republic of Ireland	1,065	1,153	265	54	153	254
India	368	436	34	9	141	140
Pakistan	294	374	10	14	158	103
West Indies	449	621	14	7	290	323

A series of community surveys followed these mental hospital admission findings in an attempt to elucidate possible reasons for the variability between ethnic

groups and factors within each subculture which contribute positively and negatively to the mental health
of that group (Cochrane 1979a). The remainder of this
chapter will be devoted to a consideration of the special features of each of the major ethnic groups in Britain and a review of the way in which these cultural
differences are likely to be related to mental health.

The Irish

People born in the Republic of Ireland constitute
numerically the largest group of immigrants in Britain.
In 1976 there were approaching 700,000 Irish-born residents of Britain, with possibly the same number again
of people born in this country of Irish parents (Commission for Racial Equality 1978). All told, up to 10
per cent of everyone in Britain has some Irish ancestry
(Rees 1982: 76). Table 9 shows that the Irish-born
immigrants in England have very high rates of admission to mental hospital and it was observed that this
is partly due to higher rates of schizophrenia but due
particularly to excessive rates of alcoholism. Exactly
this pattern has been observed wherever there have
been large numbers of people of Irish origin. In the
Republic of Ireland itself Walsh *et al*. (1980) and
Cochrane and Stopes-Roe (1979) found both of these
diagnoses produced elevated numbers of patients in
mental hospitals compared to England. Cochrane
(1977) showed that the pattern of mental illness among
the Irish-born in England was much more similar to
that of Ireland than to that of the natives of England.
However, a community survey of 200 Irish-born residents of England showed a picture of remarkable
stability and progress. In fact the Irish immigrants
exhibited fewer symptoms of psychological distress
than did a comparable native English group or a comparable group still living in the Irish Republic. It will
be necessary to return to this contradiction later.

The most common explanation given for the high rates of schizophrenia and alcoholism among the Irish is related to the existence of a set of views on marriage, the family and sexuality in rural Ireland which have only recently been supplanted by more cosmopolitan values. Murphy (1975) noted several aspects of this outlook which might have psychiatric consequences. The first of these is the way in which marriage and sexuality have been restricted. Eligibility for marriage among men in rural areas of Ireland is largely dependent upon economic independence and is therefore achieved only late in life in many cases. Because historically there has not been a system of primogeniture in the inheritance of land (Walsh 1962), farms have tended to become fragmented and only with great difficulty has it been possible for the sons of a farmer to achieve a livelihood from their own land. A very high proportion of men in rural areas thus never marry, and those that get married do so at a much later age than is typical in other countries. Walsh (1976) showed that in 1946 no less than 93 per cent of male agricultural labourers under 45 were unmarried compared to less than 50 per cent in all social groups in Ireland.

The late age of marriage and a very censorious view of sex outside marriage means that a large proportion of the population is celibate and in addition still living in the parental home well into middle age. It has frequently been reported that there is a strong association between the onset of schizophrenia and the unmarried state.

The second factor of potential psychiatric importance in the traditional rural Irish family noted by Murphy was a lack of emotional closeness between the male members of the family (father/son and brother/brother). This may be due partly to the inevitable competition for land and the importance of the extended family which devalues the position of the father in the nuclear family (Walsh 1962: 64). This basic distrust of other men extends beyond the immediate family to neighbours, workmates and friends and, it appears, can only be reduced under the influence of alcohol.

Finally, it has been suggested that there is a peculiarly intense but ambivalent relationship between mother and sons. In many rural Irish families the mother is a more powerful figure than the father and uses this power to keep their sons within the parental home even when the son would prefer to get married. The mother may, for example, interpret the sexual attraction of her son to another woman as a sign of weakness and foolishness, and thus create additional guilt in the man. In whatever culture, the picture of the dominant, emotionally blackmailing mother has been associated with a higher incidence of schizophrenia and possibly alcoholism. Murphy considers that the most promising clue to understanding Irish alcoholism is the fact that drinking always takes place outside the home but in company, 'Most Irish think of alcohol as making a man more friendly. This suggests that the Irish need alcohol in order to feel friendship or companionship for persons outside their own family, and that Irish culture does not provide and may even inhibit other means of developing such feelings.' (Murphy 1975: 132)

Obviously things have changed considerably in rural Ireland as they have elsewhere and the influence of the traditional attitudes described by Murphy and others will have only a shadow of their former power. On the other hand, it is undoubtedly the case that remnants of cultural norms and beliefs persist long after the material basis for their existence has disappeared. In any case a large proportion of the present adult population of Ireland (and of Irish immigrants to Britain) will have been socialized prior to the enormous changes that transformed Irish society in the 1960s and

1970s. In the survey of Irish-born residents of England referred to above (Cochrane 1979) the average age was 40 and the average length of residence in this country twenty years which indicates that a large proportion of immigrants spent their formative years in the Republic in the 1940s and early 1950s.

The fact that in the community survey of psychological problems Irish immigrants to Britain came out as very stable, exhibiting very few symptoms on average, is perhaps best explained by considering emigration from the Republic to be a dual phenomenon. On the one hand, the majority of migrants to Britain may come to escape the kinds of pressures that have just been described and in addition to avoid some of the economic consequences of having little or no land in a rural area. This particular group is well motivated, ambitious and psychologically stable, as is shown in Table 10, and rapidly adjust to the country in which they settle. On the other hand there is a much smaller

Table 10 Average psychological symptom scale scores found in four different ethnic groups living in England

Country of birth	Number of people in sample	Average number of symptoms	Significantly different from:
England	256	3.7	Indians, Irish
India	200	1.9	Pakistanis, English
Pakistan	200	3.2	Indians, Irish
Ireland	200	2.3	Pakistanis, English

Source: Cochrane 1979a

but statistically significant minority of Irish immigrants (usually people who migrate as young men without jobs or homes to come to in Britain) who account for the excessive psychopathology in the Irish-born community as a whole. These are people who often have originated in rural areas but perhaps tried life in Dublin prior to migrating to Britain and appear to be moving in order to escape certain personal problems centring around alcohol, but in fact bring the problems with them. This small group accounts for the overrepresentation of the Irish in mental hospitals (and also incidentally in hostels for the homeless and in prisons). For these reasons they are unlikely to figure in any community survey based on households as they are unlikely to be resident in a stable household. Even if they do have stable residences they are often unavailable for interview because of the amount of time they spend out drinking. These two groups may be quite separate and have relatively little contact with each other and indeed anecdotal evidence suggests that there is a great deal of hostility towards the latter from the former, more respectable, settled group of Irish immigrants. The high rate of psychopathology among the Irish does not therefore necessarily reflect a greater vulnerability to mental illness diffused throughout the whole Irish community but the special problems of an excessively deviant and distinctive minority on the margins of this community.

West Indians

In 1976 there were approximately 365,000 West Indian-born residents of Great Britain together with approximately another 240,000 of their dependants. This total constitutes only just over 1 per cent of the total population of the British Isles. Several of the early studies of the effects of culture upon mental health focused upon the West Indians because they were early and relatively visible arrivals in this country. Almost without exception the studies have pointed to a higher rate of schizophrenia in West Indians than in natives and this accounts for their somewhat higher overall rate of mental illness (see Table 9 for example). Some of this excessive rate of schizophrenia is reduced when age and social class corrections are applied, as schizophrenia tends to be a disorder of younger and lower social status individuals and it is in these very categories that immigrants are initially overrepresented. Unlike the Irish the West Indians are very visible as immigrants and are therefore likely to encounter prejudice directly. It is quite understandable that prejudice both in its direct and immediate form in terms of personal insults and discriminations and in the perhaps more insidious if remote form of the political activities of the National Front and British Movement is likely to have negative consequences for mental health.

West Indians typically come to this country with high expectations of achievement in terms of material wellbeing and also probably in terms of achieving integration within the wider community. Alienation results from a failure both to meet these expectations and to reach the assimilation goals that the immigrant has set for him or herself (Bagley 1975). The failure to assimilate is largely because of a strong resistance to assimilation by the host community. There is ample evidence of discrimination against West Indians in terms of housing, jobs and income (Smith 1976), and quite probably in terms of official reaction too. The alienation thus produced may become manifest in terms of individual deviance such as psychological disorders, and in political and social deviance. Take, for example, the rapid and widespread development of the Rastafarian subculture. This reflects the extent to which West Indian youths are attempting to generate a coherent and distinctive culture of their own in response to the failure of the British host culture to offer them the chance of a full self-identity within the dominant mode. The creation of a viable alternative culture may produce psychological benefits in the longer term, albeit possibly hastening the deterioration of intergroup relations which the contact between incompatible belief systems often engenders (Rokeach 1966).

One of the most noticeable features of the particular pattern of psychological disturbance shown by West Indian-born patients diagnosed as schizophrenic is the frequency with which religious delusions are manifested. As early as 1964 Kiev was commenting on the extent to which psychotic patients of West Indian origin were likely to express religious delusions, often accompanied by feelings of persecution. However, his observations were based on a sample of only ten patients. The high level of paranoia experienced by West Indian patients has also been commented on by Gordon (1965) and by Tewfik and Okasha (1965). Other commentators have gone so far as to suggest that the frequent expression of religious ideation may mean that many West Indians receive a diagnosis of schizophrenia when this is inappropriate (Littlewood and Lipsedge 1978). In a later study Littlewood and Lipsedge (1981) found that 45 per cent of Carribean-born psychotics had religious delusions. This may be linked to the exhuberant Pentecostal Christian religious groups to which some West Indians belong. These groups emphasize overt religious worship such as speaking in tongues and extensive participation in services. These activities may appear more unusual to a Western-trained psychiatrist than to a West Indian. This is not to suggest that West Indians have wrongly been diagnosed as mentally ill when in fact they are only exhibiting religious fervour. Littlewood and Lipsedge suggest that many of their West Indian patients who displayed this religious symptomatology were best described as having acute psychotic reactions with good prognosis rather than the more conventional diagnosis of schizophrenia. Many of their patients had once been regular church attenders but their attendance had begun to decline some time before the patient consulted a psychiatrist, usually because the churches did not seem to offer the satisfaction that the patient demanded. They suggest that the Pentecostal churches

> might well play a mental health role in allowing the free expression of culturally sanctioned dissociative behaviour . . . attitudes and experience which were culturally sanctioned in a religious setting appeared to become maladaptive, if not pathological, outside the framework of the church. By emphasizing the universality of man the church may perhaps offer a substitute satisfaction for failure to succeed in becoming part of the British society. (Littlewood and Lipsedge 1981: 316)

Thus this particular acute psychotic reaction may be an attempt at coping after the person finds the method provided by the culture of origin has failed and finds he is not allowed access to the prevailing British institutions.

There does appear to be some trend toward a levelling of psychological disturbance rates between those of West Indian origin and natives. Cochrane (1979b), unlike earlier studies, found that West Indian schoolchildren displayed no higher rates of behavioural disturbance than did natives. They were also functioning just as well in academic terms at school as their native counterparts. It is possible, therefore, that the second generation of West Indians may not have the same rate of psychological disturbance as the first generation immigrants.

Indians

Immigrants to Britain from India appear to be among the more successful of the recent arrivals. Not only are they less likely than natives to be admitted to mental hospitals, they also show fewer other personal and social pathologies. They tend to have lower unemployment rates than natives, a low involvement in crime and drunkenness, to live in well integrated families, in socially cohesive communities, and to show very definite signs of upward social mobility albeit often within an Indian business context (Cochrane and Stopes-Roe 1981a). The same pattern exists with the children of Indian immigrants in our studies – namely they are high academic achievers in school and exhibit fewer behavioural problems than do natives (Kallarackal and Herbert 1976; Cochrane 1979b).

The outstanding success of Indian immigrants is probably attributable to a combination of three factors. First of all there has undoubtedly been a very highly selected migration from India to Britain. Not all those who wish to migrate have been able to do so and to overcome the very strong formal and informal barriers to achieving migration the potential immigrant has to display considerable powers of ambition, ability and psychological stability. To contemplate migration in the first place, involving as it does a complete cultural transition as well as unknown hardships and dangers, implies a high degree of ambition and adventurousness. To implement the migration once it is decided upon, even obtaining sufficient finance, is also a great achievement for someone from the rural areas of India. The same characteristics which made migration possible in the first place also produce the upwardly mobile, ambitious, psychologically stable person who appears to be typical of Indian immigrants in Britain.

The second factor is a relatively supporting community and family life. Indian immigrants have been remarkably successful in reassembling their families around them upon arrival in a new country and the strength of the Asian family is well documented. The extended family and active participation in the cultural and religious life of the Indian community are also characteristic. These factors undoubtedly play a part in defending the individual against the threat of social isolation, prejudice and alienation which might otherwise jeopardize their mental health.

The third and equally important factor is the existence of a degree of flexibility in the culture of origin. Hindus and Sikhs, who form the vast majority of Indian immigrants to Britain, show considerable ingenuity and adaptability in their adjustment to the demands of life in a Western urbanized society. They manage this transition without having at the same time to abandon their cultural heritage. Indians have a reputation the world over as traders and merchants and seem to be enhancing this reputation in Britain. Reflecting the rapid adoption of host patterns of life is the fact that a very high proportion of Indian married women go to work – almost the same proportion as English married women. This not only boosts the family income but possibly provides some psychological protection for what might otherwise be a vulnerable sector of the Indian population.

The emphasis placed upon education by the Indian subculture means that many of the second generation will be academically successful and achieve upward social mobility through the channels which are normal in this country. Increasing proportions of the sons and daughters of Indian immigrants are going to university and taking their places in the professions as well as in the business world. It would seem that only a vigorous and sustained racist campaign directed at the Asian community is likely to disrupt the social integration and personal wellbeing of the typical Indian immigrant and his descendants.

Pakistanis

The Pakistanis have been conspicuously less successful in their adjustment to life in this country than their Indian counterparts. Although they have very low rates of mental illness as indexed by admission rates to mental hospitals, their average level of psychological symptoms as measured in the community survey was no different from that of the native community (Table 10). This is indicative of what is sometimes called 'underutilization' of health services facilities. Morgan and Andrushko (1977) found exactly the same pattern in Canada. They noticed that Pakistani immigrants tended to use mental health facilities at a much lower rate than did native-born Canadians, but when they were admitted to hospital tended to be admitted with serious diagnoses and stay for prolonged periods. They attributed this to the hypothesis that many Pakistanis with minor psychological problems fought shy of seeking treatment.

The Pakistanis, of course, have experienced all the same pressures of selection at the point of migration as have Indians. They too have a very supportive traditional family structure, based in this case upon the Moslem religion. However, this tradition appears to lack the flexibility of Hinduism. In a survey of 200 Pakistanis we found only six women who were at work. Presumably many of the women were prevented from working by the strictures of the Moslem tradition.

Unlike the Indians, the Pakistanis have not been materially so successful since arrival in this country. They tend to occupy the same low-status occupations that they entered upon arrival here and have not migrated upwards. It appears that the longer Pakistanis have lived in England the *more* likely they are to experience psychological problems, this being much more marked for women than for men. It also appears that those who migrated for positively material reasons (for better jobs and better living conditions) also experience more psychological difficulties. Perhaps the apparent discrepancy between the low level of mental hospital admissions and the relatively high level of psychological symptoms can be resolved by reference to the Pakistani family. It became clear in our study (Cochrane 1981), as has often been suggested previously, that people in the Pakistani community are much more strongly identified as part of a family than are the English. The Moslem family tradition may at once make it less likely that personal difficulties will be brought to the attention of outsiders for fear of bringing discredit upon the family, and may at the same time provide a high enough level of social support that such professional help is less likely to be required in any case. It has also been suggested that it is not uncommon for Pakistanis, particularly women, experiencing psychological difficulties to return to Pakistan. The return to the homeland may be initially for a holiday, to recharge batteries as it were, but may become more extended if the illness persists.

The finding that the longer Pakistanis had lived in Britain the higher the level of psychological difficulties obviously rules out any hypothesis which suggests that the actual period of migration itself produced stress which in turn produced psychopathology. The majority of Pakistani respondents in our study had maintained a strong connection with Pakistan and had a strong orientation to Pakistani culture. For example, 96 per cent of our sample communicated regularly with someone still in Pakistan and fully 60 per cent owned property there, in many cases purchased since migrating to Britain. Most significantly of all, over 60 per cent of Pakistanis expressed a desire to return permanently to Pakistan at some time in the future.

The commonest pattern of Pakistani migration seems to be that it was originally envisaged as a relatively brief and temporary relocation to accumulate sufficient wealth to be able to purchase land or property in Pakistan. It may be that as length of residence in England increases, achieving the goal of returning becomes less and less likely and symptom levels increase, especially among the women who have relatively little contact with English culture. For those who came to Britain largely for economic motives and have not met with the success they perhaps expected, the separation from the homeland and culture of origin must be doubly frustrating. Therefore this may be a situation in which the strong and rigid cultural traditions may at one and the same time be inhibiting material progress but also providing a method of coping with the psychological consequences of economic disadvantage.

Mental health and community integration

On several occasions in this chapter I have alluded to the possibility that there may be contradictory pressures on immigrants in a relatively unwelcoming society such as Britain. It may be that the goal of integration is only attainable at the expense of psychological security. Gordon (1964, 1975) has provided the basic analytical tools for studying the level of assimilation in different ethnic groups. He has also pointed out that it is quite possible for an immigrant, in whatever society, to lead many important aspects of his life within an ethnically closed grouping. Thus, because of housing and other forms of segregation, family life, religious observances, economic activities, shopping, employment, entertainment and even schooling may take place with little or no contact with the host community.

In Table 11 I have tried to assess each of the major subcultural groups in Britain for their degree of assimilation on the seven dimensions used by Gordon. Perhaps a word is in order to define some of the dimensions that Gordon suggests. Cultural assimilation or acculturation implies the greatest accommodation on the part of the immigrants to the host culture. However, even acculturation does not necessarily mean assimilation as the majority society may

reject attempts by the minority ethnic group to assimilate. Even acculturation with structural assimilation
can still be possible within quite segregated ethnic
groups. This kind of assimilation, often called cultural
pluralism, is usually considered to be an acceptable
alternative to complete integration. However, it
appears that neither cultural pluralism nor cultural
assimilation is occurring as far as the non-white subcultures in this country are concerned.

The striking feature of the material contained in
Table 11 is that there may very well be a negative
association between assimilation and mental health. It
is quite possible that the groups which are the most
isolated from the host community, both because of
prejudice and because of a desire on the part of the
ethnic minority to maintain their separate traditions,
are the least vulnerable to psychological disorders.
Thus the Pakistanis who have not achieved a high
degree of assimilation and do not appear to be moving
in this direction, even in the second generation, may
be the best protected from the psychological problems
that would otherwise come their way. The West Indians, who perhaps in the original generation have
sought integration but found it denied to them, are a
group at some degree of risk of psychological disorder
and this will extend into the second generation to the
extent that they are also rebuffed in their attempts to
integrate. The West Indians are the only group in
which the second generation show a lower degree of
assimilation than the first generation. This is because
of the deliberate creation of a counter-culture among
West Indian youths. This may further inhibit their cultural assimilation but may provide some protection
from psychological problems.

The Irish are in a somewhat different position
because they are able, if they so desire, to merge into
the host culture even in the first generation. They are
not visibly distinctive from natives and share many cul-

Table 11 Patterns of adjustment in four ethnic minorities

Type of assimilation (after Gordon 1964)	Irish		Indian (Sikh and Hindu)		Pakistani (Muslim)		West Indian	
	Generation							
	1st	2nd	1st	2nd	1st	2nd	1st	2nd
Cultural	V	V		(V)(V)			V	(V)
Structural	V	V		(V)(V)				
Economic	(V)(V)	V	(V)	V		(V)		
Marital		V		((V))				
Identificational		(V)		(V)(V)			(V)(V)	(V)(V)
Attitudinal	V	V	V	(V)(V)				
Behavioural	(V)	V		V		V	V	
Civic			V		V		V	(V)
Pattern for 2nd generation	Acculturation		Frustration		Encapsulation		Alienation	

V = Assimilation occurring
(V) = Partial assimilation occurring

tural and religious traditions. It may be, however, this very lack of a cultural distinctiveness which produces identity problems for the second generation.

Many Indians appear to have little desire for full assimilation but are able to create a successful life within their own subculture. They, too, would probably be rejected if they did attempt full integration into British society, but are able to avoid this rebuff and so escape the possible psychological consequences. However, if we look even further, beyond the immediate concerns of psychological wellbeing towards race relations, the Indian pattern of adjustment may also have negative consequences. One of the most influential theories of racial prejudice suggests that what lies at the core of much prejudice is the fear that the prejudiced-against group is in fact very different in important beliefs, attitudes and values to one's own group. It may often be possible to prove that this fear is a myth. However, if there are genuine and deep seated cultural and religious differences between groups such as exist between the English culture and the Indian culture then increasing contact between the two will produce more, rather than less, conflict. It certainly does not appear that with increasing familiarity between the two groups there is any diminution in hostile feeling. Here is yet another example of the impossible demands made on people by society. It appears that we have not yet learned how to optimize the three indisputably desirable goals – those of racial harmony, tolerance for cultural differences and individual psychological security.

Chapter 6

Stress: the case of unemployment

A case history

Mr Eric Latymer was a man in his late thirties when he was admitted to the acute ward of a mental hospital with a diagnosis of 'depressive neurosis and probable hypochondriacal reaction'. When admitted he was lethargic, tearful and very difficult to communicate with. His GP, who had been called to his house by a neighbour, feared that he might attempt suicide and had arranged an emergency visit by a psychiatrist who, although she did not think this was likely, agreed that Mr Latymer needed treatment. He had in fact been in regular contact with his GP for the previous month because of complaints of continuous chest pains and occasional very severe stomach cramps. When examined by the psychiatrist on admission to hospital Mr Latymer also mentioned that recently he had heard voices telling him to 'end it all'. The voices were not very persistent and he realized that they were hallucinations but he believed that the fact he was hearing them indicated that he was going mad.

In the months prior to the onset of his chest pains and subsequent breakdown Mr Latymer had had several misfortunes. Until eighteen months previously he had lived with his mother in a large rented house which she partly sublet to a variable number of itinerant labourers who worked on and off for two local firms on various construction sites in the city. This provided her with a small income which, when added to Mr Latymer's wages as a warehouseman at a local motor components wholesalers, provided a comfortable standard of living. Apparently Mr Latymer was reasonably content with this arrangement and had no real friends outside home. He drank heavily and fairly regularly but never to excess. He had quite frequent bouts of illness with undiagnosed stomach ailments but had otherwise been a regular worker for the three years he had been with his firm.

However, he was not well integrated with his workmates who believed he might be homosexual and occasionally taunted him about his apparent lack of sexual experience and interest.

His mother, who like Mr Latymer was a very heavy smoker and who had had a weak chest since childhood, died of lung cancer following two years of illness. Mr Latymer seemed to cope with the immediate stress quite well and as his only other surviving relative was a younger brother in a hospital for the mentally handicapped, Mr Latymer 'inherited' the rented home and five lodgers. They treated their new landlord with considerably less respect than they had his mother, frequently declining to pay any rent and sometimes physically tormenting Mr Latymer for being 'queer'. One lodger in fact accused Mr Latymer of making homosexual advances towards him and, although there was no independent evidence of this, he and a friend beat Mr Latymer badly enough for him to be detained in hospital for a night.

Following this incident Mr Latymer stayed off work for two weeks and began complaining to his doctor of chest and stomach pains and had more and more days off sick. He also took to drinking in his room rather than going out to pubs to avoid all unnecessary contact with the other men in his house.

In the November before going to hospital in March he lost his job. This was ostensibly because of a cutback in the orders received by his firm but he believed, perhaps with justification, that his recent poor attendance record due to illness counted against him. His redundancy pay was sufficient to pay the rent to his landlord which by this time was three months overdue. His mother had had no official permission to let rooms in the house but the landlord, or his agent, had turned a blind eye in return for a somewhat elevated rent.

Because of his redundancy and lateness with payments the landlord became more insistent that rent be paid on time. The three remaining lodgers in the house had all been laid off some months previously and insisted to Mr Latymer that they had no money to pay their share of the rent because they had been on 'the lump' (technically self-employed but without paying any tax or National Insurance contributions) and were not entitled to benefits. They also apparently hinted at physical violence if he became too persistent or went to social security officials for help. His own reduced income was being almost entirely spent on drink.

After missing paying the rent for two consecutive months Mr Latymer became very distressed and was admitted to hospital. It transpired that he had been admitted to a different mental hospital twelve years earlier after taking a small overdose following being sacked for petty theft from his employer. He had recovered balance quickly after a short course of ECT and with the sympathetic understanding shown by his mother. On this occasion recovery was much slower and the patient displayed a distinct reluctance to leave the hospital. His eventual discharge after seven months was followed by a readmission two weeks later following an incident when he was found by the police very drunk and having apparently taken a bottle of aspirins. His condition continued to deteriorate and the periods of hospitalization lengthened until he became a virtually permanent inmate in a chronic ward.

This case history, in which the names and some details have been changed to protect confidentiality, nicely illustrates many of the points to be made in this chapter which will concentrate on the way in which social stress might be implicated in the aetiology of mental illness. Frequent reference will be made elsewhere in the chapter but one or two points of commentary are in order here. First, although by no means a sign of pathology itself, it is unusual in our society for a man approaching 40 to be single and still living with his mother. Second, some of the psychological symptoms manifested by the person concerned may have predated the events which were the immediate antecedents of admission to hospital. Third, the locus of Mr Latymer's pains seemed to shift from stomach to chest following his mother's lung cancer. Fourth, Mr Latymer's mother, it seems, was able to run the house and keep the lodgers in check but they treated him very differently after his mother's death. The question of his sexual orientation remains unclear and is probably unimportant, but he may have appeared less competent to other people than his mother had. Finally, suspicion remained that the hallucinations reported by the patient may have been invented by him, although the depression itself was real enough.

The nature and importance of stress

Many of the factors considered earlier in this book (such as social class and gender) can only have an indirect effect on mental health. Their impact must be mediated by some other variable and the one to which reference is most often made is 'stress'. The assumption of an intervening variable between social situations and pathology has been made since earliest times. In its simplest form, for example, the pattern of connections between antecedent, intervening and dependent variables is conceived of as follows:

Low social status → more stress → psychopathology

This kind of model was employed in the studies of Langner and Michael (1962) in New York. It quickly became apparent that the introduction of a simple intervening variable was insufficient either to account for the variability observed in the empirical data or to be conceptually satisfying. The case history at the opening of this chapter shows that other factors such as pre-existing vulnerability, personal and social resources and the availability of alternative responses have to be considered in addition to the occurrence of stressful events.

The problem has also been one of explaining how external social and material situations get translated into internal psychological and psychosomatic responses. The usual way of dealing with this question has been the implicit assumption of a 'black box' into which go external stimuli (stressors) and out of which come psychological responses. The black box assumption has even been made explicit at times (e.g. Rahe *et al.* 1974). More recently the concept of stress has become grounded in potentially observable psychophysiological reactions which are believed to have psychological consequences.

Sterling and Eyer (1981) reviewed a great deal of the more recent evidence on the mechanisms by which stress can produce adverse consequences and developed a model based upon the well-known arousal response. When a person perceives an external material or social threat the brain automatically prepares the body for activity (the 'flight or fight' response, as it is sometimes known). This is done by suppressing anabolic processes (such as synthesis of protein, fats and carbohydrates for growth, energy storage and bodily repair; production of white blood cells for the immune system; sexual processes, etc.) and increasing catabolic processes (energy mobilization by breaking down protein, fats and carbohydrates; increased production of red blood cells to carry oxygen; increases in blood pressure; decreased sexual processes, etc.). However, this only prepares the person to respond to stress in a physical fashion; what the brain also has to do is to instil a suitable motivational state for these preparations actually to be used. This motivational state is anxiety. Now if the arousal produced by stress can be employed effectively this provides a very positive physiological and psychological outcome. In fact many people deliberately seek arousing experiences (sport, films, love, etc.) in well circumscribed situations with which they know they can cope, and we all derive satisfaction from overcoming problems and difficulties. The point is, however, that in many circumstances the stress encountered in daily life in our society cannot be controlled effectively by the flight or fight response. Chronic physiological arousal can lead to a variety of pathological consequences such as hypertension, heart disease and even cancer (Sklar and Anisman 1981) but, equally, long-term and unrelieved mental arousal may lead to psychological problems like neurotic anxiety, alcoholism, depression and possibly psychoses.

Obviously, the mere occurrence of stressful events is not a sufficient explanation for the average increase in the risk of mental illness which has been shown to be associated with exposure to high levels of stress. What is required to begin to account for the differential effects of stress on different people, and in different contexts, is a model such as that in Fig. 3. Parts of this model, which is presented in a purely abstract form in the figure, will be illustrated in the subsequent section on unemployment and extended and amplified in the final chapter of this book.

If we re-examine the case history of Mr Latymer with the model as a guide some salient issues are brought out more clearly. The immediate stressor (job loss) occurred in the context of other recent events (mother's death, assaults, money problems) which had not been successfully resolved, so perhaps was likely to be perceived as particularly threatening. At the

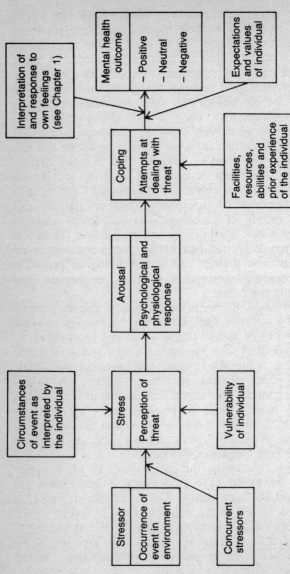

Fig. 3   A model of stress, coping and mental health

same time Mr Latymer might have been particularly vulnerable, as evidenced by his apparent inability to establish an identity and existence independent of his mother. We may assume, therefore, that Mr Latymer was at a high level of arousal and extremely anxious and, because of his sheltered life, low level of education, lack of coping skills and friends to turn to for help, he quickly exhausted all the resources which might have enabled him to deal with the immediate problem. His previous responses to his inability to cope involved turning to his mother and to symptoms of physical illness, but in this case these were not effective either and consequently he became exhausted and depressed. It also appears that his expectations about the quality of life were not very high and presumably he was not unduly distressed by the prospect of prolonged hospitalization.

Stress and mental illness

If we stand back for a moment and ask what relationship, if any, has been discovered between life stresses and psychological distress we are, for once, confronted with an apparently straightforward answer. The many dozens of studies carried out in this field consistently point to the existence of a moderately strong relationship – in correlational terms the magnitude is about $+0.3$ (Cochrane and Sobol 1980). Typically, studies compare a group of patients with a diagnosed mental illness and a matched group of non-patients and ask each about the kinds of events that have befallen them in the previous year. Sometimes the level of stress encountered is elicited through a semi-structured interview but more frequently with a standardized checklist of events such as the Life Events Inventory (Cochrane and Robertson 1973) which is included as Appendix 2. Inventories such as this are psychometrically simple devices whereby the items are derived from a variety of sources and then each is weighted by asking samples of patients and non-patients to rate the event on a standard scale for the amount of distress and disruption they believe its occurrence might cause. These weights are averaged and then used in the subsequent scoring of the inventory – a total score being derived for each respondent by summing the weights of the events which have happened to him in the previous year (or whatever other period is used).

The attractions of such a measurement device are obvious: it enables rapid, economical and in some senses standardized assessments of the experience of the more common stressors to be made in a wide variety of contexts. There are also disadvantages, of course, particularly the absence of any assessment of the meaning of an event to the particular person who experienced it. However, it is true to say that the outcomes of studies using simple inventories and those using more elaborate techniques are virtually identical: they almost invariably show that people with psychological problems have been exposed to significantly more stress in the period immediately before the assessment is made than have those without problems. This seems to be true whether the researcher is interested in undifferentiated mild neurotic symptoms (Cochrane and Stopes-Roe 1977; Dohrenwend, B. S. 1973; Garrity *et al.* 1977; Phillips 1968), depression (Lloyd 1980a; Markuch and Favero 1974), schizophrenia (Brown *et al.* 1973; Jacobs and Myers 1976), attempted suicide (Cochrane and Robertson 1975), anxiety (Vinokur and Selzer 1975) or a range of physical health problems.

The exceptions to this overall pattern can be as instructive in their own way, as can the large measure of agreement found. There are situations which objectively seem to be producing very high levels of external and relatively uncontrollable stress (wars, civil insurrections, imprisonment in concentration camps, expulsions from homeland) but which may not produce commensurately high levels of psychological disturbance. To take but one example; the situation in which a large part of the population of Northern Ireland have found themselves in the last decade or so might reasonably be assumed to have produced continuing stress levels unapproached for a large segment of the population in this country since the bombing of towns and cities in the Second World War. Many people have had first-hand experience of bombing, rioting, shooting, harassment and even of having relatives maimed and killed. Yet what research there is seems to suggest that there has not been a detectable increase in most forms of mental illness (Fraser 1971). Indeed, one study at least has shown a real decrease in the rate of depression in the areas most adversely affected by civil disturbances (Lyons 1972). Why is it then that the perhaps minor events such as those recorded on life event inventories seem to bear a consistent relationship to psychological distress whereas occurrences of much greater magnitude may not?

One answer may be found in what Coser (1956) called the positive functions of conflict. Where distressing events are shared community experiences their negative impact may be offset by increased group cohesiveness and social interaction consequent upon dealing with the stress. In addition, new roles and statuses will emerge in the crisis, social isolation may be reduced and there will be some distraction from strictly personal worries. Perhaps most important of all, the people involved can attribute any sense of anxiety or malaise they have to external causes and do not have to resort to explanations based on personal illnesses and inadequacies. It is very unlikely that experiencing a personal tragedy such as divorce or a bereavement will have any such positive side-effects.

The otherwise impressive consistency of the results in this area should not be allowed to obscure the fact that many questions still exist about the nature of the relationship which has been demonstrated. Several of the most important of these issues have been brought to the fore by the important work of George Brown and his colleagues in London and it will be a valuable prelude to subsequent discussion to review some of this work.

In a major study of the role of life events in the aetiology of depression, Brown and Harris (1978) compared several groups of women from Camberwell in London. The patient sample consisted of 73 psychiatric inpatients and 41 outpatients with a diagnosis of depression uncomplicated by other conditions. A comparison group of 458 women, randomly drawn from the same community, was also selected and interviewed by sociologists and in some cases by psychiatrists. It was found that a high proportion – 36 per cent – of these women also had psychiatric problems. They also were mainly suffering from depression and from this group two further samples were taken – definite cases and borderline cases – leaving a total normal group of 295 women.

In the year before the interviews the psychiatric patients and the community cases had experienced many more severe life events than had the normal women but, interestingly, the rate of less severe events did not differentiate the groups. When the content of the severe events was examined it was found that the crucial element was that of loss. Events involving separations from, and deaths of, friends and relatives, loss of employment, loss of an important relationship because of unfaithfulness and loss of a home were the crucial events in producing depression. There was evidence, too, that the occurrence of other severe events in addition to the first increased still further the risk of depression.

It is at this point that many studies conducted before that of Brown and Harris ended. In this case, however, the authors took it as a beginning and went on to explore other aspects of the relationship between life events and depression, two of which will be examined in some detail as they have been taken up by other researchers.

The problem of causality

As is frequently pointed out, the existence of a correlation does not demonstrate causality. In the present context it is equally plausible to explain a high rate of disruptive life events in terms of them being brought about by a disturbed personality as it is to attribute psychological disturbance to the occurrence of the events. It may indeed be a symptom of incipient mental illness that the sufferer's life becomes severely disrupted. It also remains possible that a third, and perhaps hidden, factor is responsible for the variation in both disruptive events and psychological distress. The kind of factors that come to mind are genetic predisposition or personality characteristics formed in childhood.

Two ways of tackling this problem have been suggested. The first, which attempts to establish the independence of events from the action of the patients, has not been particularly successful. It turns out that for only a few of the things that happen to people can we be absolutely certain that they were not influenced by the person's own behaviour. The death of a loved one is an example of such an event. The episode of unemployment which featured in the case study described earlier, on the other hand, may very well have been partly brought about by the illness of the person involved.

Brown *et al.* (1973) and Brown and Harris (1978) have tried an alternative approach which involves the careful dating of the actual onset of illness (as opposed to onset of treatment) as well as the occurrence of the stressful events. Clearly, if an event precedes in time the first appearance of a disorder then it cannot be caused by that disorder but is more likely itself to be a causal agent. In addition, the shorter the time interval between a distressing event and the subsequent onset of illness the greater the likelihood of there being a causal relationship between the two. Brown satisfactorily demonstrated that the incidence of severe long-term loss events preceded the onset of illness in the women with depression he found in his community samples in Camberwell. He also demonstrated that the incidence of these events was most marked in the few weeks prior to the onset of depression – in other words, the high rate of occurrence of events was not a continuing feature of the lives of these women, therefore there was very good reason for believing that a truly causal relationship existed.

Even if it is accepted that life stresses play some causal role in the aetiology of psychological disturbances, exactly what the impact of stress causes to happen remains problematic. One hypothesis is that stress can cause a person to experience an episode of psychological disorder that they would otherwise not experience. But there is another possible type of causal relationship that is sometimes referred to as the 'triggering' hypothesis. Brown was among the first to suggest that life events may bring forth something that was going to happen sooner or later anyway because of a strong pre-existing tendency towards disorder in the person concerned. In other words, the occurrence of stress is not a sufficient explanation for a disorder but may be useful in explaining why it happened *when* it did.

If this latter hypothesis were correct then it would not be necessary to posit that people with psychological problems had experienced more stresses than people without problems, just that they responded to stress more violently than did the normal group. Brown and Harris (1978) made use of this assumption to estimate whether events were causing depression in the stronger meaning of the term. On the basis of the relationship between the rate at which stressful events befell people in the general population and the proportion of patients experiencing stress within a given period, they were able to estimate the nature of the relationship. The specific measure they used was a 'brought forward time' index which is effectively an estimate of how long it would have been before a particular person would have become depressed (by random selection alone) had not a stressful event befallen them. A short period would indicate that life stresses were triggering something that was about to happen anyway and a long period indicates that stress was causing something to happen which probably would not have happened otherwise. (The brought forward time is *not* a measure of the interval between events and onset.) In the study already described, Brown and Harris found that the hypothetical brought forward time was two years for the depressed patients and just over two years for the cases they found in the community (Brown and Harris 1978: 123). These lengthy periods are much more compatible with the idea that severe stresses are truly causal of depression rather than just triggering an episode.

Lloyd (1980a, 1980b) reviewed a number of studies that looked at the nature of the relationship between life events and depression. She found that some people were predisposed to depression by childhood stresses (especially the death of a parent) and were two or three times more likely to become depressed as adults than those without these experiences. However, most adult depressives will not have experienced this childhood stress and are not vulnerable in this way. Lloyd further estimated that severe recent stresses are more directly predictive of adult depression than is the vulnerability factor and therefore her work supports the conclusions of Brown and his colleagues.

Although it is well accepted that life events do cause depression the same cannot be said for other psychological disorders. Brown applied his 'brought forward time' analysis to schizophrenic patients also (Brown et *et al.* 1973) and found that the effect of stresses was, for most patients, merely to trigger an episode that would probably have occurred within a few weeks in any case. Day (1981), in a careful review of the 'triggering' hypothesis in relation to schizophrenia, does point out, however, that although on average the results of most studies support this notion it is only true for a minority of all schizophrenic patients that a serious event befell them immediately prior to the onset of a schizophrenic episode. Most episodes occurred in the absence of any easily identifiable 'trigger'. Both Lloyd and Day point to the need for prospective rather than retrospective studies in the search for the nature of a causal link between stress and mental illness.

Intervening variables – social support

It has been observed several times already that not everyone who experiences a stressful event will respond with psychological disorder – indeed, only a small minority of those experiencing quite severe stress actually break down. Several researchers have addressed themselves to this issue of what distinguishes those who can apparently cope with stress from those who cannot.

It became clear quite early in the history of life-stress research that the social context of the person was likely to be related to their vulnerability. Myers *et al.* (1975) found that people who were unemployed, unmarried and generally dissatisfied were more vulnerable to the effects of stress than were those who were married, at work and well integrated socially. Particularly well protected were those people who had 'ready and meaningful access to others' (Myers *et al.* 1975: 426).

Brown, among others, took up this notion of the availability of social support as an intervening variable between stress and mental illness. In his study on depressed women in Camberwell he found that the existence of an intimate confiding relationship was a very potent protective factor and its absence made the women involved much more prone to depression in the face of stress. After encountering severely stressful events only 10 per cent of women became depressed if they were involved in a close and supportive relationship with someone else (not necessarily a sexual relationship), whereas over 40 per cent of women experiencing the same degree of stress but without the protection of such a relationship became depressed within one year.

This finding has now been replicated many times and in many different contexts and it has until recently been the unchallenged wisdom that what we are dealing with is an interaction between stress, social support and illness such that the right kind of social support can mitigate the effects of stress. Recently, however, it has been suggested that perhaps social support is a positive predictor of good mental health, and its absence a predictor of poor mental health, whether or not stress is present.

Williams *et al.* (1981) report one of the few longitudinal studies of the relationships between stress, social support and mental health. Longitudinal studies are particularly valuable because they make possible a more direct causal analysis of the interactions between the variables included than do even the most sophisticated cross-sectional studies. Williams *et al.* used data gathered from a sample of over 2,000 people living in Seattle, Washington in order to test two competing models: a simple additive model and an interactive model. The former hypothesized that stressful life events and the absence of social supports would each have an independent negative effect on mental health: the latter predicted that the negative impact of life stresses would be mitigated by the availability of adequate social support. (This is the model of the relationships supported by the work of Brown and Harris and generally assumed by most other investigators.) Each participant in the Seattle study completed two similar questionnaires at a year's interval which measured mental health, social support, life events, physical illness and a variety of sociodemographic characteristics. By controlling for initial mental health levels the researchers were able to judge the effects of changes in social support and life stresses on mental health one year later. They found no evidence at all for the better known interactive model – the impact of life events was not modified by social support. Such supports made a positive contribution to mental health whether or not the person was experiencing stress. The simpler additive model was quite sufficient to account for their results. Incidentally they found that the best single predictor of mental health was the level of mental health as measured a year previously. This, perhaps not unexpected, finding must lead to great caution in any causal interpretation of the relationships that have been found between life events, social supports and psychological disturbance in cross-sectional studies – the relationship could be causal in any direction.

Although other studies, too, (e.g. Andrews *et al.* 1978; Holahan and Moos 1981; Lin *et al.* 1979) have produced results which suggested the independence of the positive effects of social support from the negative effect of life events on mental health, at present it is not possible to be categorical that these factors are totally independent of each other. Indeed, Pearlin *et al.* (1981) suggest that the effects of social support are more subtle than were initially believed in that they do not directly intervene between stressors and psychopathology but may nevertheless be important in maintaining positive self-esteem which in the longer term may be an important psychological advantage. It is impossible not to agree with these authors when they say that 'Clearly, the understanding of the functions of coping and supports requires more than their conceptualization and measurement . . . research into social supports would seem to be in the very early stages of its development . . .' (Pearlin *et al.* 1981: 350–51).

Unemployment

Rather than attempt a comprehensive survey of the literature relating stressors to mental illness it is intended to concentrate on just one example of an experience which is often thought to have stressful implications – unemployment.

The reasons for choosing unemployment as the example are numerous. First, there is its obvious topicality. In 1982 the number of unemployed in Britain hovered around three million and most analysts predicted further increases in the level in the future. Unemployment is also at the highest level it has reached since the Second World War in the rest of the EEC and the USA. Second, unemployment is universally placed on lists of events that are designed to measure stress and in most cases it represents a definite break in a person's life with a precise date of occurrence.

Unemployment is a relatively clearcut event which lends itself to study more readily than do perhaps the more diffuse stressors (such as marital discord or financial difficulties). A further advantage in this respect is that official agencies collect and disseminate a wide range of statistics about the occurrence and distribution of unemployment within the population – something which cannot be said for most other stressful events. As one would expect, therefore, a considerable body of empirical work relating unemployment to mental illness is available for examination.

The third reason for concentrating on unemployment is somewhat the opposite of the advantages just listed. Unemployment research illustrates very well many of the difficulties and pitfalls of attempts to relate stress and psychological disorder. The question of causality is particularly important as all the evidence available clearly shows that unemployment is not a random event with everyone having an equal probability of being affected. From the case history, Mr Latymer could be viewed as having brought about his own unemployment because of psychological instability which predated his redundancy. If this were to happen with any great frequency a cross-sectional study which simply compared the mental health of the employed and the unemployed might erroneously conclude that it was unemployment which was causing mental illness. Fontana *et al.* (1972) cite a striking example of a person who apparently deliberately engineered his own unemployment as a strategy for coping with other ongoing life stresses which were, to him, more salient than having a job. This form of unilateral manipulation of interpersonal relationships by deliberately provoking crises may be a common strategy among those people with fewer alternative coping resources (see Chapter 8).

Research in the 1970s showed that even prior to a particular episode of unemployment the unemployed were far from typical of the working population as a whole. The left hand column of Table 12 summarizes the major differences between the employed and the unemployed. It can be seen that these same factors

Table 12 Characteristics of the unemployed

Characteristics which may exist prior to a particular episode of unemployment (cf. the employed)	Characteristics which have been attributed to the effects of unemployment
More psychological problems	Psychological problems
Poorer physical health while at work	Poorer physical health
Lower wages while in work	Loss of sense of purpose
From disturbed or broken families	Poverty
	Family tensions
Lower qualifications, lower skilled	Negative self attitudes
Older	Feelings of degradation
From larger families	Inertia, laziness, boredom
More frequent job changes	Lower ambition, work seen as less attractive
Previously experienced unemployment	Political resentment
More likely to have had an unemployed father	Susceptibility to fascist ideology
	Social isolation

may be directly related to both the likelihood of unemployment and the likelihood of mental illness. In a correlational or cross-sectional study a causal link between unemployment and mental illness might be derived because of the confounding of variables antecedent to both conditions. Even when, as in the 1930s and 1980s, a major cause of unemployment is mass redundancy and workplace closure brought about by distant economic forces rather than personal job losses through sacking, there is still reason to believe that redundancies are more likely to hit people who have these characteristics. Obviously, with increasing overall levels of unemployment and more and more people being affected, the employed and unemployed populations will overlap to a greater extent in terms of the distribution of other variables. It remains true that definitive studies would need to match the employed and unemployed groups on the characteristics in Table 12 in order to be able to attribute any psychological effects directly and unambiguously to the experience of unemployment.

The other major source of methodological problems in the study of the consequences of unemployment is that, for most people, it is synonymous with poverty. It is not perhaps a very startling finding that when people find their income drastically reduced they should become worried and unhappy; but most researchers want to go beyond this and say that the loss of a job is much more than simply the loss of an income. While this may accord quite well with intuitive feelings it has proved very difficult to demonstrate unequivocally.

Finally, while listing the values of using unemployment as an example of stress there is the obvious fact that people respond very differently to what on the surface appears to be a very similar experience. If a factory closes down and makes 1,000 people redundant, only a small proportion will become psychologically disturbed. Some might manifest some of the other effects attributed to unemployment which are listed in the right hand column of Table 12. Others, perhaps the majority, will show no discernible effects at all beyond a decline in spending power and a restructuring of their daily life. The most interesting question then becomes – what is it that makes people react so differently? This is a question to which we will return towards the end of this chapter.

Why should unemployment be considered stressful?

Although most people readily assume that unemployment is unpleasant and potentially harmful to those who experience it, one might be forgiven for questioning this belief. In jokes, at least, work is often considered, along with marriage and death, as probably inevitable but something to be avoided if at all possible. One of the advantages of being wealthy is that work is not essential and many people fantasize about inheriting, or winning, large sums of money which would mean that they could give up their job. Most people look forward with positive anticipation to their retirement which they believe will free them from the constraints of work and allow them to spend more time doing what they would rather have been doing all along.

Obviously, for most people working is inextricably bound up with money – 'earning a living'. In fact, in Britain people without jobs still receive an income which enables them to survive in some degree of comfort, and surveys have shown that the overwhelming majority of people say that they would continue to go to work even if they did not have to (Warr 1982). This result should be evaluated in the knowledge that in most cases this remains a purely hypothetical question until retirement. Working provides most people with an income in excess of what is required barely to sustain life and allows some indulgence in non-essential activities and consumption.

Beyond these material considerations both social scientists and laymen alike seem to believe firmly that being in formal paid employment has desirable psychological consequences for the individual and that being out of work will, in many cases, lead to psychological problems. For the layman the reasons for these consequences may be couched in relatively simplistic terms – 'the Devil makes work for idle hands'. Jahoda and Rush (1980) have described five 'latent functions' of employment which, although they may be seen as by-products from a strictly economic perspective on work, may have very important psychological consequences:

1 Work imposes a definite time structure on the working day.
2 Work compels people to come into contact with

people outside their immediate family environment.

3 Work demonstrates that there are goals beyond the individual and which require collaborative action.

4 Work confers a certain status and an aspect of social identity (e.g. carpenter, lecturer).

5 Work compels people to be more or less active.

Jahoda and Rush contend that only paid employment ensures that all of these functions are met. Housework, charitable work, hobbies and leisure pursuits *might* provide one or more of them but only a 'contractual arrangement involving financial rewards' forces these experiences on people. 'Of course one can work without a contractual arrangement, of course one can engage in leisure activities, but the absence of social compulsion in such activities requires a degree of initiative from individuals which only few psychologically privileged human beings can muster on a regular basis.' (Jahoda and Rush 1980: 12).

Unemployment, or indeed not having a paid job out of choice because of wealth, children or retirement, means that these latent consequences of employment are likely to be absent. Further, it is assumed that their absence will be psychologically destructive. This is a rather limited view, however, of the latent consequences of unemployment and employment. It is based on a value judgement that work is a good thing because activity, status, collective action, social contact and a well-organized life are good things. Jackson and Stafford (1980) showed that for a sample of school-leavers the lack of employment only had negative psychological consequences if they also had a high 'work involvement'. This was reflected in such things as feeling that having a job is important, that work gives purpose to life, and a belief that boredom is an inevitable consequence of unemployment. For those with low work involvement the consequences of not having a job were far less dramatic. For youngsters in employment a low level of work involvement was associated with *poorer* mental health compared to those with a high degree of commitment to work.

In the same vein Warr (1982) has pointed out that for many people having a job is itself a source of stress which might in some cases be reduced by unemployment. Warr estimates that perhaps 5 per cent of all employees are, at one time or another, under severe work-related strain and some are likely to become seriously affected. Indeed, although the majority of people say they would like to continue working even if there was no economic necessity, a majority of those in work also say that they would like to change their current job. It seems that we are perhaps more enamoured with with idea of work in the abstract, and not so keen on it when the alarm rings in the morning and we face the prospect of another day actually doing it.

One further point before embarking on a review of the research on unemployment and mental illness: retirement for many people has many of the same features as unemployment, including financial losses, and yet most people who have studied retirement conclude that it is relatively unproblematic and that a lowering of the retirement age might actually be beneficial. Most retired people when asked what they miss about work reply 'nothing'; an American survey showed that less than 20 per cent of retired men missed any aspect of their previous work. Kasl (1979) in reviewing the vast literature on retirement concluded that there was no good evidence to suggest the transition from work to retirement was associated with any adverse effects on physical or mental health. Why should there be this discrepancy between the impact of retirement and the impact of unemployment? Surely the answer lies in the social definition of the two status categories rather than in any intrinsic differences in the actual experiences of the unemployed and the retired.

Unemployment and psychological disturbance

As in most other areas of psychiatric epidemiology, there are two distinct methods of investigating the hypothesized link between unemployment and mental illness. One tradition has relied upon aggregate statistics relating to mental hospital admissions and unemployment levels while the other has used the community survey to elucidate the nature of the relationship.

Brenner (1973, 1976) has produced the most extensive and best known aggregate studies. He used employment statistics for the years 1914 to 1970 in the USA to predict subsequent changes in a whole range of statistics relating to physical and mental health. In his report to the Joint Economic Committee of the United States Congress, Brenner showed what the effects would be of an increase in the rate of unemployment of 1 per cent if this were sustained for five years (Table 13). What the table shows are the additional pathologies in 1975 produced by an increase in the level of unemployment from say 4 to 5 per cent in 1970, assuming that unemployment stayed at 5 per cent during the intervening five years. Interestingly, he found that equivalent changes in other economic indicators (such as the rate of inflation) did not have such direct effects.

In Britain unemployment rose by 1.6 per cent, from 4.1 per cent to 5.7 per cent between 1975 and 1976 and has remained above this level ever since. If we extrapolate directly from Brenner's USA data to Britain (and this begs a lot of questions) the consequences in 1981 directly attributable to this sustained increase in unemployment would be roughly as follows: 280 additional suicides; 2,700 additional mental hospital first admissions; 6,000 additional imprisonments; 36 extra murders; 15,000 additional alcoholics; and 18,000 additional deaths due to all causes. It is important to realize that these figures (and those in Table 13) take no account either of any subsequent rise in the unemployment rate which would produce additional increases in the incidence of the listed pathologies, or of the undoubted effects of the initial 1 per cent rise in unemployment in the years before and after the fifth year chosen for these examples.

Table 13 The impact of a 1 per cent increase in unemployment sustained for five years in the USA

Pathology	Change in rate (%)	Additional cases	Approximate cost of additional cases (1975 prices) ($ million)
Suicide	+ 4.1	920	43
Mental hospital first admissions	+ 3.3	4,227	55
Prison admissions	+ 4.0	3,340	210
Homicide	+ 5.7	648	434
Alcoholism (cirrhosis deaths)	+ 1.9	490	N/A
Total mortality	+ 1.9	36,887	6,600

Source: Adapted from Brenner 1976

The statistical methods used by Brenner are extremely complex and the extrapolations above give a somewhat oversimplified picture of his results and conclusions. He found, for example, that changes in the unemployment rate were more predictive of mental illness for some groups than for others – indeed for some groups (the most poorly educated in particular) *lower* levels of unemployment were associated with increased rates of mental hospital admissions. Equally, Brenner's work has not been without its critics, although these are divided over whether better data would produce results which are easier to interpret, whether alternative controls such as mental hospital capacity need to be considered (Marshall and Funch 1979), whether the results of Brenner's study are replicable (Marshall and Dowdall 1982), or whether Brenner's analysis can be applied in Britain (Gravelle *et al.* 1981).

There has been only one full-scale replication of Brenner's study of unemployment and mental hospitalization rates in Britain. Stokes (1981) used exactly the same procedure as Brenner to analyse the relationship between statistics for England and Wales for the period 1950 to 1976. He, too, found a positive correlation between unemployment levels and mental hospital admission levels but the relationship was weaker than that reported for the USA. The adverse effects of unemployment seemed stronger for women than for men and were only evident in specific age groups (35–44 for men and 20–24 for women) although a case could be made out that these two age groups have maximum involvement in the economy for the two sexes respectively.

It is perhaps worth stressing that these aggregate data studies do *not* demonstrate that it is the actual individuals who become unemployed who appear on the other side of the equation in the mental illness statistics as well. Indeed, Brenner thinks this is unlikely to be the entire explanation for his findings. What we are dealing with here are rather global indices of economic activity and social pathology in the total population. It may very well be that only some of the extra psychopathology occurs among those directly affected by unemployment but other people will be affected in other ways by the economic downturns indexed by unemployment rates. The wives of unemployed men and those workers whose jobs are made insecure by a decline in economic activity are but two of the most obvious categories of people also likely to be subjected to additional stress when unemployment is on the increase.

Catalano and Dooley (1977) tried to find out what was the effect on the lives of individuals when community level measures of the unemployment rate varied. They analyzed the results of interviews conducted with 1,100 people in Kansas City spread over a sixteen-month period. Using this method they calculated the average level of depressive symptomatology and life stresses for each calendar month reported by those respondents interviewed during that month and related these variables to a variety of ecological economic indicators. They found that an increase in the regional unemployment rate was followed in the next month by increased reporting of life events. Two to three months later still the level of depression in the community had also increased substantially. As is usually found to be the case, life events and depression were themselves positively correlated. In a follow-up analysis of these same data Dooley and Catalano (1979) were able to demonstrate that it was not only job-related life events which increased as community unemployment levels went up – non-economically related stressors were also reported with greater frequency. Men (whether in work or not) appeared to be affected more than women by increases in unemployment and the lowest income groups were particularly responsive to economic changes. These studies showed conclusively that fairly soon (8 weeks) after unemployment levels rose the average psychological state of the community as a whole began to deteriorate.

Several recent studies have compared the psychological status of the unemployed with those in employment. In the survey of the factors contributing to symptom levels among the general population in England carried out by Cochrane and Stopes-Roe

(1980a) and already referred to in earlier chapters, it was found that being unemployed was one of the main determinants of poor mental health. Unemployment had a greater impact on symptom levels than did any of the other demographic variables examined in this study. There was a greater difference in the symptom levels of unemployed men and their employed counterparts than there was for women; however, the wives of men who were unemployed had extremely high levels of symptoms showing that they were being indirectly affected by their husband's unemployment. Cross-sectional studies such as this are not able to distinguish between psychological symptoms which may have predated unemployment and those which were a consequence of unemployment. What is really required is a longitudinal study of people both before and after they become unemployed and then, if possible, a continuation to assess the effects of differing lengths of unemployment on psychological state.

Fortunately several such studies have been carried out. Kasl and his colleagues (Kasl *et al.* 1975; Kasl 1979) interviewed 113 men whose factory was about to be closed. The initial interview was carried out about 4–7 weeks before closure and there was a series of follow-up interviews conducted at 5 weeks, 5 months, 1 year and 2 years after the closure. Also included was a control group of men from comparable companies who had not lost their jobs. In this study an enormous amount of data was gathered on both physical and mental health as well as on economic problems. Although it was found that men who became unemployed were more depressed than the control group, this elevated level of depression was evidenced in the anticipation phase of the study (i.e. before the factory had actually closed) and the difference between the employed and the unemployed group did not get progressively greater over time. In fact there was some evidence of a diminution of depression in those men who remained unemployed for a considerable length of time. When comparisons were made on the other aspects of mental health there were no differences between the employed and the unemployed group and on the measure of psychophysiological symptoms the unemployed were actually *better* off than were the employed.

Pearlin *et al.* (1981), also in the United States, made use of data from a longitudinal study of 2,300 people who were interviewed twice at a four-year interval. A number of people in this study lost their jobs between the first interview and the second. It was clear that those who became unemployed also became significantly more depressed in the intervening period. However, losing a job had many other effects apart from influencing the level of depression. The experience of unemployment also influenced the degree of satisfaction expressed with the marriage, the success of the parent/child relationship, and brought about, as might be expected, economic difficulties. In fact, adding the effects of these longer term role strains to the immediate effects of job loss produced a much better prediction of the eventual level of depression found at the follow-up interview.

In Canberra, Australia, Finlay-Jones and Eckhardt (1981) carried out a very well designed study of 400 young people who were unemployed. They interviewed these people and administered a short version of the Goldberg General Health Questionnaire (GHQ) (Goldberg 1972) to assess their level of psychological disturbance. They found that fully 56 per cent of their sample scored at the level which indicated that they had a serious psychological disorder, an assessment which was subsequently validated in interviews conducted by psychiatrists. During these interviews it was possible to ascertain that only 30 per cent of the 'cases' had onsets before their experience of unemployment. The remaining 70 per cent had become seriously disturbed psychologically since they had become unemployed, although some of them had experienced other stressful events in addition to unemployment. The median time-lapse between unemployment and the onset of psychological disorder (mainly depression) was about five months. For the unemployed sample as a whole, 'caseness' rate as detected by the GHQ was about three times the Australian national average based upon community surveys taken from the population at random.

In Britain several investigators have concentrated on the effects of unemployment on youngsters. Stafford *et al.* (1980) interviewed 650 young people just after leaving school, all of whom were poorly qualified youngsters with less than two 'O' levels to their credit. In this study, as in the study by Finlay-Jones and Eckhardt, the GHQ was employed, although in this case the 12-item version rather than the more reliable 30-item version was used. Stafford *et al.* found that those people who were still unemployed 7 months after leaving school had significantly higher scores on the symptom scale, but in addition were more likely to come from families where the father was also unemployed. This same sample was followed up eight months later (Jackson and Stafford 1980) when they were reinterviewed. Using this method it was possible to assess the effects of either finding or losing employment in the intervening period. Those who were initially unemployed but who had gained employment showed a large drop in their symptom levels, whereas exactly the opposite was true for those who were initially employed but who subsequently lost their jobs. Those who had remained unemployed for the whole period did not show any further decline in their mental health. It should be noted that those who were in employment initially, but who subsequently became unemployed, did have high symptom level scores at the initial interview. It must be presumed that they were either unhappy because their jobs did not suit them or, perhaps, they lost their jobs because of their relatively high level of psychological instability. The interaction found between unemployment, psychological symptoms and the factor of work involvement has been commented upon earlier in this chapter.

Finally, two studies conducted by Stokes (1981) are worthy of mention here. In his first study Stokes looked at the effect of unemployment on adults made redundant when a factory closed in Bradford. He followed each of the sample of unemployed men and women who agreed to participate for six months after their initial redundancy and he compared them with a sample matched on socioeconomic status, sex and marital status who had remained in employment. He found that the unemployed had significantly higher levels of psychological distress and also felt more hostile and guilty. In addition they were less satisfied with themselves and reported more family and marital dissatisfactions. However, Stokes found that with increasing experience of unemployment there was if anything a slight *improvement* in the wellbeing of the people concerned. This improvement was most marked for married women, who may have had a viable alternative role available. In his second study, using the same design, Stokes looked at the effect of prolonged unemployment on Birmingham school-leavers. He compared 47 youngsters who left school without jobs and 47 who left school with jobs, for a period of six months. As with the adults, the unemployed youngsters had higher levels of psychological disturbance, were more hostile and more likely to feel rejected, but again it was found that over the period of the study the mental health of the unemployed youths improved somewhat and they became more self-accepting.

The fact that there may be a tendency for people experiencing prolonged unemployment to adapt to their situation is not necessarily wholly healthy. What was happening in the case of Stokes' youngsters, for example, was that they were not bothering to apply for jobs, staying in bed late and had abandoned any hope, or even desire, of ever finding employment. This feeling was graphically summed up by one unemployed youth who said 'I'll probably get a job one day. But until that time comes I'm not too bothered.' The reduction in anxiety level, as indexed by the low scores on the symptom scale, in fact may have made it less likely that the person concerned would ever get a job.

Why are some people affected by unemployment more than others?

Not everyone who becomes unemployed experiences deleterious psychological consequences. Indeed, the rate of psychological stress produced by unemployment may not be all that much greater than the rate of stress produced by certain kinds of employment. As with any other kind of stress, the effects of unemployment will vary according to the social and personal circumstances of the individual experiencing it. Reference back to the general model of the stress process presented earlier in this chapter will indicate some of the areas which it may be profitable to examine in order to map out the reasons why some people respond adversely and others do not.

Just as not all jobs are equivalent, not all experiences of losing jobs will be equivalent. Jobs vary considerably in their characteristics and their ability to provide satisfactions for the person doing them. We would expect someone losing a high-status job which involved pleasant working conditions to feel more deprived by its loss than someone who derived little or no status from his job and found his working conditions boring and unpleasant. In attempting to explain the relative ease with which factory workers adjusted to redundancy, Kasl (1979) concluded that

> what may tax the adaptive capacity of blue collar
> workers in low skilled jobs may not be job loss or
> retirement as much as it is coming to terms with the
> dull, monotonous job in the first place. If most workers
> adapt by giving up any expectations that work will be a
> meaningful human activity – and thereby compromise
> their positive mental health – then we should not be
> surprised that the loss of the work role among such
> disengaged workers may not be the trauma which facile
> generalizations from the stressful life events literature
> would seem to dictate. (Kasl 1979: 195)

Even in jobs which are not inherently dull, monotonous and dehumanizing there is still often a potential for stress. In the 1960s and 1970s there was a small movement of people away from what they considered the 'rat race' to a more tranquil form of existence. These were people who were very often in well-paid, highly skilled occupations but which they nevertheless considered to be in some way incompatible with positive mental health. Such people voluntarily gave up their jobs to live in remote rural areas in search of values other than those associated with work and careers.

Jobs will also obviously vary tremendously in the degree to which they provide the latent satisfactions contingent upon being in employment. Most surveys of what people like about their jobs suggest that the provision of social contact and a sense of achievement is very important. If a person's main source of these gratifications is via their employment we would expect job loss to be more traumatic than it would be in the case of someone who has alternative sources of these satisfactions outside their employment. All of these things will combine to produce circumstances surrounding the particular event which will make the individual more or less likely to interpret it as stressful.

If we turn now from characteristics of the job that

is lost to characteristics of the individual made unemployed a further range of possibilities opens up. As the work of Stafford *et al.* cited earlier has shown, people vary considerably in the degree to which they are involved with work. Some people will find a major part of their self-definition, and hence their self-esteem, in terms of their occupation. This is more likely to occur at some stages in a career than others and will be influenced by other aspects of the person's life which he or she considers important in this respect. The origin of the work-involvement ethic probably lies in the subcultural environment in which the person was brought up and is influenced by his subsequent experiences at work. It has been suggested that we have recently witnessed a diminution of the work ethic in general in our society but hard evidence to support this view is so far lacking as surveys of the unemployed show that the vast majority would prefer to be at work. Indeed, the responsiveness of unemployment statistics to other economic indicators suggests that the major determinant of unemployment is not changes in attitude of the workforce but more remote economic forces.

The context in which unemployment takes place will also be very important. A person who loses employment because of mass redundancy will have a better explanation for his misfortune than will the person who is singled out from among his colleagues for dismissal. The attribution of an event to external factors, and sharing the same experience with many other people, may work to mitigate the effects of that event. It is also often true that where mass redundancies occur the opportunities for finding alternative employment are commensurately low and associated anxiety that much greater.

We also need to consider the prevailing social definition surrounding unemployment. If the unemployed are seen typically as scroungers and workshy then the person made redundant may be more vulnerable to a loss of self-esteem. If, however, unemployment is socially defined as being independent of the activities of the people affected, or an alternative social definition is available, such as early retirement, then losing a job may be less threatening. For these reasons it may therefore be somewhat easier to bear unemployment at a time when unemployment levels are high than when unemployment is a relatively unusual phenomenon.

The model (see Fig. 3) also directs our attention to concurrent stressors which may accompany the target event (in this case job loss). Some of these concurrent stressors may be partly contingent upon unemployment. It is obvious that most people who become unemployed will also experience financial difficulties, although these may be delayed for some time by redundancy payments and other benefits offered by the company or the State. It has been suggested that the period immediately after losing a job, when people typically have some redundancy payment to spend and have planned to undertake many activities which were previously impossible because of their work commitments may be a relatively troublefree, indeed even happy, time. This period is inevitably shortlived and the reality of having to seek re-employment at a time when this is perhaps very difficult soon asserts its influence upon the person's psychological state.

There are undoubtedly other concomitant life changes when a person is faced with unemployment. In a study by Cohn (1978) on the effect of unemployment on self-esteem, it was found that the self-dissatisfaction brought about by unemployment was considerably accentuated if it was accompanied by a change in role position within the family. Thus, men who were made unemployed fared worse if their wives were still in employment. In other words, if there was a large decline in the proportion of the family income contributed by a man then he would feel the effects of unemployment more acutely. On the other hand, if he remained the major breadwinner (albeit on a reduced income) the effects were less traumatic. Equally, it was true that men who took up a range of housework tasks when they were made unemployed also experienced a decline in self-esteem.

A related finding from this same study was that people who have a clear alternative to the work role were not as badly affected by unemployment as were those who did not have this alternative. Cohn found that men, and women without children, were much more likely to suffer negative consequences than were women with children. Motherhood offers a socially validated full-time role which fatherhood does not. The absence of a clearcut alternative to employment increased the individual's vulnerability to the stresses of unemployment.

The extent to which the experience of unemployment produces stress is obviously very variable and contingent on many other factors. So far discussion has focused on the translation of a 'stressor' into stress and it has revealed a very complicated process, but one which is only half the story. We also have to consider the variety of ways in which people can respond to stress if and when it is experienced as such. The application of this half of a complete model is the subject matter of the final chapter of this book.

Chapter 7

Social reaction, labelling and mental illness

The concept of mental illness has been used somewhat loosely throughout this book and yet the use of such a term carries many implicit assumptions. The most important of these assumptions is that which lies at the core of modern clinical psychiatry – namely that there is a therapeutic advantage to be gained by regarding psychological problems as analogous in some way to physical illness. The use of the 'sickness' analogy, or more generally the medicalization of psychological and behavioural problems is a relatively recent phenomenon (Szasz 1970). It arose for a number of reasons, all of them understandable in a historical context. First, there was the undoubted success that was being achieved by physical medicine in dealing with the problems with which it was confronted: those dealing with psychological problems perhaps wanted to achieve the status and effectiveness of medical practitioners. Second, there was the discovery that certain mental conditions did in fact have a physical basis – notably that general paralysis of the insane was the result of an earlier infection with syphilis. This led to an assumption, which is still widespread, that all mental illness eventually would be traced to an underlying biological cause, whether it be biochemical or genetic. Third, there was the undoubted desire on the part of many psychiatrists to improve the treatment of the insane. The improvement was produced by gaining something of the special status and tolerance reserved for the physically ill for those with psychological problems.

Although the development of the medical model of psychological problems is understandable, what is not perhaps so readily apparent is that the adoption of this analogy carries with it certain problematic implications as well. There is, for example, the tendency to forget that the notion of 'mental illness' was developed as an *analogue* of physical illness whereas it is now often accorded exactly the same scientific status. This means that there is the implicit adoption of a universal standard of mental health from which any deviation is inevitably, and perhaps biologically, pathological. This fails to take account of the fact that there might be quite significant cultural differences in what is regarded as normal and abnormal in terms of behaviour – variations which probably do not occur in the case of physical illness. Diabetes, malaria and tuberculosis have a similar expression wherever they exist and are always regarded as undesirable conditions. It becomes relatively easy to categorize anyone whose behaviour deviates from the prevailing standards as mentally ill rather than as just different. A diagnosis of illness carries with it the obligation to try to restore the unfortunate sufferer to health – in other words to seek conformity rather than to tolerate innovation.

A second unintended consequence of adopting the medical model of mental illness is that the overt manifestations of psychological problems are regarded as merely indicators of something else which underlies them. They may be considered as symptoms which enable a diagnosis to be made, but are not in themselves the real problems. Just as with a physical illness, the suppression or control of symptoms may be relatively unimportant until the underlying cause is identified and cured. Thus there is a reification of what began as analogy into an actual existence of a disease which then becomes more important than its behavioural expression. A person is no longer considered to be someone who has delusions but is a 'schizophrenic', with all the implications that label carries.

Finally, and perhaps most importantly of all, the over-reliance on the physical disease analogy produces an orientation to therapy which is basically physical. Thus the most commonly used, and some would argue the most effective, treatments so far developed for the major psychological disorders are based upon drugs or other attempts to modify biological functioning, such as ECT. All of these forms of treatment have been developed in advance of any clear idea of *why* they should work. In the case of schizophrenia, for example, the progression has been from the discovery of an effective biochemical treatment to an analysis of biochemical differences between schizophrenics and normals.

As the reader will undoubtedly be aware, there has recently been a considerable reaction against the dominance of the medical model in psychiatry. Thomas Szasz (1960) has declared that mental illness is a myth, R. D. Laing (1967) has argued that schizophrenia may be a mask behind which individuals hide their real personal problems, and others have not been slow in following their lead. Psychologists in particular have been attracted to the alternative views of psychological problems to those proposed by psychiatrists. However, the prevailing psychological model is only different in superficial respects to the medical model. Psychologists have substituted the notion that the causes of a disorder are to be found in the learning history of the individual rather than in his biology, and have suggested that rather than physical therapy some form of resocialization is likely to lead to the most desired out-come. This outcome remains, however, that of return-ing the disturbed individual to conventional behaviour and to a state of personal comfort.

The labelling theory of mental illness

The most coherent, radically different approach to the medical model of psychological disorder has been developed by sociologists using the social psychological concepts of symbolic interactionism. A core assump-tion of symbolic interactionism is that our self-identity arises out of our own interpretations of our social intercourse with other members of society. In large part we come to know who we ourselves are by seeing what other people make of us and by making sense of the way in which they act towards us: 'Human nature, mind, and self are not biological givens; rather, they emerge out of the process of human interaction.' (Manis and Meltzer 1978: 6) Although these basic ideas were formulated many years ago, it is only rela-tively recently that they have been applied system-atically to the study of deviant identity as well as to the study of normal identity formation.

Credit for the development of the labelling theory of deviant behaviour is usually given to Howard Becker. In a book published in 1963 called *Outsiders* he brought together many important insights into the way in which society can contribute to the production of deviance within the individual. Becker was not merely restating the traditional sociological view that the causes of deviance are located in social forces but that, '*social groups create deviance by making the rules whose infraction constitutes deviance*, and by applying those rules to particular people and labelling them as outsiders.' (Becker, 1966: 9) The radical departure was to suggest that deviance was not a quality of the act but a consequence of labelling. In other words, the behaviour that the so-called deviant person exhibits is irrelevant; what is important is the fact that it has been observed, or suspected to have occurred, and categorized as deviant by someone else. It is equally important to notice that the labelling perspective suggests that *who* is labelled depends not on how they behave but on their social characteristics. Finally, what is labelled is arbitrary and can change from time to time and place to place. By extension from the symbolic interactionist perspective the suggestion is that being labelled, in other words being regarded as different by important other people, has serious consequences for the self-identity of the person so labelled.

The tremendous dislocation from the normal pattern of explanation required by the labelling paradigm is nowhere more apparent than in the case of mental illness. Scheff (1966), in developing a formal labelling theory of mental illness, suggested that the behaviours which are usually regarded as symptomatic of mental illness are a residual category of deviance which is left over when other forms of explanation have been exhausted.

If a particular type of behaviour cannot be explained away as criminal, drunken, bad manners or eccentric, then this residual category is invoked. At some stages in history the residual category has variously been considered to be the result of witchcraft or possession by the devil but the current residual category we use is that of 'mental illness'.

The so-called symptoms of mental illness do not contravene the written laws of society or even rules that are clearly specified and understood, such as those governing good manners. Rather they are things such as hearing voices or seeing visions that no one else can see, inappropriate affect (in other words disagreeing with the majority about the emotional context of a particular event), being excessively withdrawn from social intercourse, experiencing intense emotions such as depression without an appropriate environmental stimulus, and so on. Witnessing these kinds of behaviours and emotional states can be both discomforting and inconvenient. It has become expedient to develop a concept which accounts for their occurrence, an appropriate and humane response, and a set of institutions designed to minimize the inconvenience by removing the individuals who cause it from society and suggesting ways in which they may be returned to more conventional behaviour. Once institutions such as mental hospitals and the people who staff them, psychiatrists, psychologists, nurses, orderlies and so on are brought into existence, they acquire a momentum and an existence which is very hard to reverse.

Scheff explains the development of chronic 'mental illness' in individuals by a series of hypotheses which can be summarized as follows:

1 Psychological symptoms can develop for a variety of reasons, e.g. organic, psychological stress, defiance, etc.

2 The occurrence of psychological symptoms will be much higher than the recorded rate of mental illness would suggest.

3 This is because on many of the occasions on which psychological symptoms are manifested they are not witnessed by others, or are interpreted in some other ways.

4 There is a common stereotype in our society of what the role of the mentally ill is.

5 People who become formally labelled as mentally ill are not initially distinguishable in terms of their psychological state from many who do not become so labelled. They are labelled because of the visibility of their symptoms and their particular social position.

6 Once a person has become labelled he will be rewarded for adopting the role of the mentally ill and punished for trying to escape from it.

7 *Labelling is the single most important cause of chronic mental illness*. This is because the labelling of an individual who exhibits deviant behaviour as mentally ill tends to stabilise or reinforce that pattern of behaviour. If, on the other hand, exactly the same initial behaviour is either not labelled or defined in some other way, such as due to intoxication, then it will more than likely be transient and not come to affect the person's self-identity.

In Scheff's model some people came to play the role of mental illness in ways which are very similar to the ways in which other social roles (such as student, father, bank manager) are acquired. A mixture of formal and informal learning of role requirements goes on both before and after the role is assigned – a rough stereotype of mental illness is available to all but on assuming the role more detailed and precise definitions and requirements are quickly learned.

Labelling theory draws a distinction between the initial occurrence of residual deviance, which may have a range of aetiologies, and the process of coming to occupy a stable role of mental illness and the consequential change in self-identity which goes along with it. Labelling theorists are in fact only concerned with the development of 'secondary deviance' and have little to say about the origins of 'primary deviance' except to note that it is widespread. It is central to the labelling perspective that the labelee adopts the proffered label for himself and as an integral part of his self-image – it is not just the reaction of others which is affected by the labelling process.

The mental hospital is suggested as the major institution in which this identity transformation is achieved and psychiatrists are the chief personnel involved. The psychiatrist is the agent of society charged with the responsibility of formally applying the label of mentally ill and the hospital provides the environment in which the labelled individual can learn his new identity. Obviously others might try to label people mad and it is not absolutely essential for a person to be admitted to a hospital for them to come to this conclusion about themselves. Nevertheless, admission to a mental hospital and diagnosis by a psychiatrist are at the core of many patient careers.

The empirical evidence for and against some of the central components of labelling theory will be examined so that an assessment of its usefulness can be made.

Is there such a thing as mental illness?

One of the crucial differences between the labelling perspective and the medical model is that while the latter reifies the concept of a disease underlying psychological symptoms the former denies that there is any such thing as a mental illness in this sense, rather it is simply a role that some people occupy.

A major piece of evidence often adduced in favour of this position is Rosenhan's famous study, *On Being Sane in Insane Places* (1973). It may be recalled that in this instance Rosenhan succeeded in obtaining mental hospital admissions for several of his collaborators who were in fact sane but were diagnosed as insane – usually as schizophrenic. He achieved this by asking each of his collaborators to present themselves at a mental hospital and complain of hearing a voice in their head saying such words as 'hollow' or 'thud'. They presented no other abnormality except to complain of this particular symptom and, as far as was consistent, gave veridical answers to the questions that the psychiatrists asked of them. All the people who went to hospital in this way were admitted and in the majority of cases were diagnosed as schizophrenics. They remained in mental hospitals for an average of 19 days before their eventual discharge; in one case the length of residence was 52 days. During this period they displayed no symptoms of insanity whatsoever and again as far as possible gave truthful answers to any questions. In not one single instance was the pseudo-patient suspected as being anything other than genuine by a member of the medical or nursing staff. On the basis of these data and the systematic observations made by the twelve pseudo-patients during their stay in hospitals, Rosenhan concludes that even for trained psychiatrists it is impossible to distinguish the sane from the insane in psychiatric hospitals.

For obvious reasons this study made an enormous impact when its results were first published. However, with a more systematic evaluation of the methods used and the conclusion reached a more balanced view of the value of the study is now available. Millon (1975) Spitzer (1975) and Weiner (1975) among others have all pointed out that Rosenhan's conclusion that we cannot distinguish the sane from the insane is not clearly proven by his study. What in fact Rosenhan demonstrated was that a number of psychiatrists failed to distinguish between the insane and people acting or feigning insanity – this is rather different to his actual conclusion. While requesting admission to the hospital the pseudo-patients certainly did not act completely sanely because they complained of hearing voices. Even while they were in hospital and actually denying the existence of symptoms the pseudo-patients' behaviour can hardly be defined as sane in the usual sense. They did not ask for release from hospital and they did not inform the staff of the real purpose of their seeking admission in the first place. Most people would consider that that behaviour was tantamount to deception if not directly feigning insanity.

It may also have been that the design of the study, which was intended to reduce the overt level of psychopathology displayed by the pseudo-patients, in fact created the condition where a diagnosis of schizophrenia was most appropriate. The pseudo-patients did not mention any situational abnormalities or severe stress experiences, and their life histories were by and large quite normal. Nevertheless they reported hallucinations and actively sought admission to hospital. At the same time they were told not to display any particular nervousness or to be upset. The combination of hallucinations without an obvious environmental cause and the lack of anxiety at having these bizarre symptoms meant that the admitting psychiatrist probably had no alternative diagnosis available other than schizophrenia. Equally, while the fact remains that most of the patients were discharged with a diagnosis of 'schizophrenia in remission', and this implies that a label had been affixed to them even after their symptoms had disappeared, it should be remembered that there was no obvious reason for the change in their state which had apparently taken place. On admission they were hearing hallucinations, after admission the hallucinations had quickly disappeared. The staff at the hospital were probably misled into believing that the illness was internally generated and its natural history might produce a recurrence of the previous symptoms.

Although Rosenhan (1975) replied to many of these criticisms they are sufficiently well-founded to reduce the status of his study from the crucial test of the labelling hypothesis it purported to be to an interesting but flawed account of life in a mental hospital. Many of the incidents reported by the pseudo-patients during their stay in the hospitals are probably more revealing than the major findings of the study. They described, for example, that they were treated not as real people by the psychiatrists and other staff but as patients. This meant that their legitimate and quite reasonable requests and questions went unanswered or were answered in an entirely inappropriate way. On most occasions when the pseudo-patients asked a question of a psychiatrist or a nurse the member of staff concerned did not respond at all but averted his eyes and moved on. On only 6 per cent of the occasions recorded did the psychiatrist actually stop and talk to the patient. Over 1,400 questions were addressed by the twelve pseudo-patients to the staff in the hospitals they attended and less than 60 of these questions were answered.

These and other subsidiary findings from Rosenhan's study do lend support for what can be called the 'weak' version of labelling theory. This version suggests that very many of the activities and institutional arrangements set up for dealing with people who are considered mentally ill are counter therapeutic: that is, they may have negative, and possibly unintended, consequences for patients. However, this is very different from saying that labelling *causes* most chronic mental illness. The most that can be said for the weak version of labelling theory is that labelling may make the process of recovery more difficult and may alter the perception of others towards the person so labelled. The weak version of labelling theory leaves untouched the assumption that there is a reality to most mental illness.

Other people have approached the question of whether mental illness really exists in very different ways. Murphy (1976) looked at anthropological evidence gathered from both her own systematic observation of the Eskimo and the Yoruba of Nigeria and a review of published sources in social anthropology. She found that the Western concept of schizophrenia was a recognizable syndrome in many other cultural contexts. Not only did such things as hallucinations, delusions, speaking to imaginary people, feelings of persecution and inappropriate affect occur in other parts of the world, but they were often grouped together by observers and taken as an indictor of some underlying psychopathology. It is true that there were culturally specific symptoms which were often attached to this common core (such things as drinking urine among the Eskimo and believing that one smells bad among the Yoruba, for example) but the syndromes were sufficiently similar to be recognized as conforming to what in the West is called schizophrenia. However, other behavioural patterns which we label neurotic were not recognized elsewhere in the world. Many similar symptoms exist among the Eskimos and Yorubas but they never formed together into a syndrome or cluster with the implication that there was some underlying disease. Thus a person who was excessively anxious or compulsive would only be described in terms of those symptoms rather than being assigned to a specific labelled category. Thus while there is some support for the notion of schizophrenia as a disease entity there is very little support from cross-cultural studies for the idea that neurotic illness is universally recognized to exist.

The third area which has been explored in this context is the proposition that mental illness is a social role. The implication here is that most people in society recognize the role of mental illness and have got at least some idea about the kind of behaviour expected of those playing it. On several occasions it has been suggested that there is a stereotype of mental illness which is constantly reinforced by fictional portrayals and by descriptions of the mentally ill in the mass media. Jones and Cochrane (1981) measured the extent to which a stereotype of the mentally ill actually exists in Britain. They took the ten symptoms which were most commonly found in a study of people in mental hospitals by Zigler and Phillips (1961) and mixed them up with a number of other characteristics and then asked a sample of the general population to say which of these applied to the mentally ill and which to normal people. They found that there did exist a definite stereotype of mental illness and of what was considered normal behaviour. Most of the actual psychiatric symptoms found by Zigler and Phillips formed part of the stereotype of mental illness and none of them formed part of the stereotype of normality, therefore there was a clear indication that the stereotypes commonly held about the mentally ill are reasonably accurate in the sense that the stereotype corresponds to the actual symptom patterns found in patients. However, the most frequently observed symptom of all in mental hospitals – depression – did not appear in the general public stereotype of the mentally ill. What was probably occurring was that the stereotype held of the mentally ill in general was, in fact, more appropriate to just one category of mental illness, namely schizophrenia, which in this country accounts for less than a fifth of all admissions to mental hospitals.

This poses a serious problem for labelling theory. If the commonly held stereotype is accurate in that it reflects one particular disorder and yet that disorder is relatively uncommon, one is forced to ask how labelling can account for the majority of episodes of mental illness which do not fall into that category.

Behaviour regarded as symptomatic of mental illness is widespread

The labelling theory has as a premise the idea that the behaviour exhibited by the person destined to be labelled is largely irrelevant to the labelling process because it is much more widespread than the incidence of recorded mental illness would suggest. In other words, very similar behaviours are exhibited by people defined as normal and abnormal – what differentiates the two categories is the reaction of important observers. Here labelling is on much stronger ground than it was when we were considering the evidence for the existence of mental illness. The numerous survey studies already reviewed in the course of this book have almost all revealed a very much higher incidence of psychiatric symptoms in the general population than would be suggested by an examination of treated cases. In the Midtown study, for example, fully 23 per cent of the population were considered by psychiatrists to be mentally ill although only 5 per cent were receiving treatment and only a further 20 per cent had received treatment in the past. The overwhelming majority of people who were considered clinically to be mentally ill had never received any treatment. More recent studies, such as that of Schwab *et al.* (1979), indicated that neurosis, depression, phobias, paranoia and alcoholism were substantially represented in their random sample of non-patients. There were at least 10 per cent of the population in each of these categories (although the categories overlapped considerably).

In our study of the distribution of psychological symptoms in urban areas of England we found that fully 36 per cent of the sample interviewed had four or more of the 22 symptoms asked about – a level which is sometimes used as a criterion for psychological 'caseness'. Over 20 per cent met the more stringent criterion of 7 or more symptoms (Cochrane and Stopes-Roe 1980a). These proportions are obviously far in excess of the proportion of the population receiving psychiatric treatment.

In their systematic analysis of over 40 (mainly American) studies of untreated psychological disorder Dohrenwend and Dohrenwend (1969) found rates reported of up to 60 per cent of the population surveyed, depending largely upon the method of deciding which respondents were cases and which were not.

Observations have been made of the attempts by husbands (Sampson *et al.* 1964) and wives (Yarrow *et al.* 1955) to explain away, or accommodate to, the deviant behaviour of their spouses in order to avoid having to consider them mentally ill. The well partner made strong efforts to interpret the behaviour as normal or the result of strain and transitory situational influences. Often it was only when the behaviour became physically dangerous or impossible to cope with that a psychiatrist became involved. Both these studies relied on samples of men and women who had eventually been diagnosed as mentally ill. Presumably there is a large number of cases where the coping strategies of the family prevent this label being applied even in the face of quite disturbed behaviour.

In reviewing much of this material Gove (1980) makes the suggestion that although there might be overlap between the behaviour of patients and non-patients, the patients as a group exhibit many more symptoms on average than do the non-patients. Adherents to the labelling perspective could quite easily counter this observation by asserting that patients have more symptoms because they are patients and have been induced by labelling to play the role of the mentally ill which includes *inter alia* having psychiatric symptoms.

There is little doubt then that what are sometimes considered psychopathological symptoms are spread far beyond the category of those who are identified as being mentally ill. Clearly there must be some other factor intervening between the presence of symptoms and the label of mental illness being applied.

Social power determines who and what gets labelled

Of course labelling theory goes far beyond merely stating that psychological symptoms are relatively common. It also rests on the assumption that there are systematic reasons, other than deviant acts, why some people are labelled as mentally ill and others are not. As the label of mental illness carries a certain stigma and may have unpleasant consequences for the person so labelled it is to be expected that people will in general wish to resist the imposition of the label as far as possible. It follows that those with more resources, in terms of power, influence, money and social contacts, will be more successful in resisting the label than those without these resources. A number of studies have been undertaken to test this hypothesis. An early study by Wenger and Fletcher (1969) in the United States assessed the effect of being represented by legal counsel at a hearing to determine whether a person should be compulsorily admitted to a mental hospital. In their assessment the people who were and were not represented by lawyers displayed equal levels of psychopathology. However, the committal rate of the two groups was very different. Of the 15 people who were legally represented 11 were not committed, of those who had no lawyer 61 out of 66 were committed by the court. Given, as Wenger and Fletcher assert, that there was no discernible difference in the mental state of the two groups of people, this seems to be strong evidence that being able to afford the services of a lawyer is a crucial variable in determining involuntary mental hospitalization. Of course, far more people go to mental hospitals on a voluntary basis but even in these cases there may be different degrees of pressure exerted upon individuals to conform to the wishes of their relatives and other advisers. The ratio of involuntary to voluntary admissions increases as we go down the status hierarchy (Rushing 1971), so that in America, at least, a higher proportion of poorer people who are admitted to hospital are admitted against their will than are the well-to-do.

There are considerable differences between the situation in the United States and in Britain. The differences extend both to the legal processes surrounding commitment to a mental hospital and the apparent interaction between the psychiatrist and patient. In his original study Scheff (1964) looked at the way in which people in America were screened for involuntary admission. To meet the legal requirements for involuntary admission a person had either to be dangerous to himself or others or severely impaired and incapable. Scheff examined the court proceedings for 163 patients who were all eventually committed to mental hospitals. On the basis of the psychiatrists' ratings of these patients he found that fully 63 per cent of them met neither of the two legal criteria, although all were sent involuntarily to mental hospitals. He attributed this to the strong presumption of psychiatric illness made by psychiatrists and subsequently made by courts. The average time taken for the psychiatric interview was only about 10 minutes and the average length of the court hearing was less than 2 minutes. In fact the court hearings turned out to be rather a sham as in every single case where a psychiatrist recommended commitment this was endorsed.

However, a very similar study in Britain by Bean (1979) found quite different results. He accompanied eight psychiatrists on all their emergency and domiciliary visits. Bean found that only 18 per cent of the people visited by psychiatrists were compulsorily admitted to mental hospitals, a further 43 per cent sought voluntary admission, but almost 40 per cent were not admitted at all. Most of those who were admitted clearly met the provisions of the Mental Health Act 1959. The length of time taken by the psychiatrists to arrive at their decision was also considerably longer than that found in Scheff's study.

In one of the few other studies that directly examined the effect of social characteristics of potential patients on psychiatrists' judgements Lebedun and Collins (1976) asked forty-six psychiatrists to evaluate written case summaries which contained indicators of the potential patient's symptoms and information on his social class, occupational and educational levels. These status indicators were randomly assigned to different case summaries so that different psychiatrists were reading the same symptoms attributed to people with different social characteristics. Lebedun and Collins found quite clearly that people who had low status characteristics (that is low educational level and low occupational status) were far more likely to receive a severe diagnosis from the psychiatrists than were people who were at the other end of the occupational/educational scale. It would be important to discover if these findings could be replicated in Britain as they do represent some considerable support for this part of the labelling hypothesis.

Finally, it is worth mentioning one study whose results are congruent with the medical model of mental illness rather than the labelling perspective. Gove and Howell (1974) suggest that the medical model would predict that those with more social power would have more access to mental health care facilities when needed than those with less social power. The labelling hypothesis is exactly the contrary to this – namely that those with social power will use it to resist being referred to psychiatric agencies. They examined the social background of 250 patients admitted to a state mental hospital with a view to ascertaining how long it had taken the person to receive treatment after the appearance of symptoms. They found that the richer a person was the more quickly he sought and received treatment. For example, among the wealthier patients in their group only 38 per cent had had their symptoms for a year or more before hospitalization whereas almost 60 per cent of the poorer patients had been suffering for this length of time. At admission to the hospital only 22 per cent of the richer patients were considered to have severe symptoms compared to 45 per cent of the poorer patients. In other words, the poorer a person was the more likely he was to be severely disturbed before he received treatment. Richer people were able to initiate their own treatment before their disturbance became severe. Gove and Howell conclude that the medical model receives far more support from their findings than does the labelling model.

The negative effects of labelling

At the core of labelling theory is the assumption that once a person is labelled both the reactions of others towards him and, eventually, his own self-perception will be more or less permanently changed. This change will be such that he becomes identified primarily with a deviant role – in this case mental illness. This identity will override most of the other identities the person previously had and become a sort of master status. These changes are inevitably quite difficult to detect directly as they require some assessment of the perception of others and self-perception prior to, during, and after the labelling process. Nevertheless, several researchers have made an attempt to examine the direct effects of labelling.

In several studies Kirk (1974, 1975) showed that people who exhibited behaviour which is usually taken as indicative of mental illness were rejected by others. There was a direct correlation between the severity of disturbance attributed to a particular person and the likelihood that he would be socially rejected by his peers. However, Kirk found that the rejection of the mentally ill was primarily if not entirely dependent upon their *behaviour*. Attaching a psychiatric label to behaviour that was otherwise normal did not appear to result in rejection: even though people believed a psychiatrist had labelled someone as mentally ill, if their behaviour did not appear to indicate this there was no negative reaction. It seems, therefore, that it is the appearance of psychological symptoms themselves rather than the knowledge that the person has been labelled as mentally ill which conditions our responses. However, it is probably true that in most cases those who are labelled do display some evident symptoms of mental illness so that the issue of distinguishing between the relative impact of the label and the symptoms on the judgements of others is largely irrelevant.

Turning to studies which have tried to look at the consequences of labelling on the self-image of the labelee we meet something of a paradox. Most patients who have been in mental hospitals clearly believe that their stay there helped them deal with their psychological problems. They also frequently show some improvement either in clinical symptoms or in their social functioning, or both, after a stay in a hospital. Labelling theory would predict that time spent in a mental hospital would produce deterioration in terms both of psychological symptoms and ability to readjust to other social roles. It is perhaps not possible to evaluate the effect of mental hospitalization by asking the patients themselves directly about it since if they have fully accepted their role as mentally ill then they would be induced to believe that mental hospitals were therapeutic as part of their socialization into this role.

Doherty (1975) divided patients in a mental hospital into those who had completely accepted their role as mentally ill and those who continued to deny that they were mentally ill even after attempts had been made to label them as such. Using both staff ratings and objective personality tests, he found that the people who rejected the mental illness label improved more quickly than those who accepted it. Indeed, the acceptors were hospitalized for a considerably longer period on average than were those who denied or rejected the role which was offered them. At one level this is clear support for the labelling hypothesis that becoming involved with the role of mental illness tends to be counter-therapeutic. However, Doherty's study was only possible because a proportion of patients were able to resist accepting the role that psychiatrists attempted to make them play. Thus labelling cannot work exactly as has been suggested if it is possible for people who are in fact institutionalized successfully to deny that they are mentally ill.

Clearly, then, labels will only be adopted by the person to whom they are applied if he or she is in a suitably receptive frame of mind. Rotenberg (1974, 1975) has addressed himself to this issue more directly than has any other investigator. He suggests that labelling will only be effective, in the sense of persuading the labelee to accept the label, if the label is consistent with the person's own prior self-conception and if the label fits a general category that the person is predisposed to accept. The first of these conditions is met when the individual has a confused or perhaps negative idea of himself. As this may often be the case among people who come to the attention of psychiatric agencies then they may be unusually receptive. Rotenberg's second point relates more to cultural differences than individual differences but may also be operative at the personal level. Labelling by someone else can only ever be successful if the person so labelled believes in the categories used. Rotenberg suggests that in our culture, at least, there is a generalized belief in what he calls *a priori* categoric ascription. This means that we have a general belief that our true personality is relatively invariant even though our behaviour may be quite variable. In other words, it would be quite consistent for someone to be persuaded to believe that they are 'schizophrenic' even though for most of their lives they have behaved quite normally. They would attribute their intermittent episodes of bizarre behaviour to the fact that deep down they have always belonged to the category of schizophrenic. Rotenberg suggests that in other cultures where the equivalent concept of schizophrenia is believed to be a more transitory state then people who are labelled in this way will only have a transitory disorder. Here, however, where the underlying notion is of schizophrenia as a permanent category from which there may be a temporary symptomatic recovery but no cure, people who accept this label for themselves are destined to become chronically mentally ill. The study citied in an earlier chapter by Murphy and Raman (1971) which showed that the course and outcome of schizophrenia was far better in Mauritius than in Britain seems to support Rotenberg's hypothesis. Where the prevailing cultural belief is that people do recover from schizophrenia then that tends to happen, but where the prevailing belief is that it is an incurable disease then people tend to enter into a long-term career of illness.

We cannot leave this section without reference to a very important study carried out by Carol Warren (1974). She examined situations in which what are usually considered stigmatizing social labels were deliberately used to produce not more deviance, as labelling theory predicts, but more conventional behaviour. The most clearcut example of this is Alcoholics Anonymous where participants are forced to accept the label of 'alcoholic' for themselves. In this situation, however, a clear distinction is drawn between the identity, which remains deviant, and the behaviour, which may or may not be deviant. Thus there is the concept of a non-drinking alcoholic. In fact, Alcoholics Anonymous deliberately uses the enforced acceptance of a deviant label to produce conventional behaviour as it persuades its members that because they are alcoholic they can never drink again, even in moderation. Although difficult to assess statistically, this strategy seems to achieve a certain degree of success. This is directly contradictory to the labelling notion that persuading someone that he was in fact an alcoholic would produce an escalation of alcoholism rather than a reduction.

Warren went on to try to analyse the conditions under which the deliberate use of a label can produce less, rather than more, deviance. She discovered that there were two factors which were necessary to prevent the escalation of deviance upon the ascription of a label. First, the labelee had to be a voluntary participant in the mini-social system which produced the label. Thus people who were labelled as alcoholics while in prison would not be expected to show the improvement that people who participate in Alcoholics Anonymous may show. The second factor was that the labeller had to be a member of the labelled category, too. If the person applying the label described himself as a member of the same category (alcoholic) then this seemed to have an entirely different effect to that caused when the label was applied by an official, an expert, or someone in authority not belonging to the deviant category. Of course the latter is usually the case in psychiatric institutions. The person doing the labelling is separated from the labelled category by their formal and informal statuses and it is rare to find a psychiatrist who has had, or will admit to have had, an episode of mental illness himself. In fact there are very few occasions on which both of Warren's criteria for a positive outcome for labelling have been met. She identified Alcoholics Anonymous, equivalent drug treatment schemes and certain weight-loss groups as meeting these criteria but most other institutional arrangements for dealing with deviance remain, in her view, likely to escalate the problem rather than reduce it. Her study does, however, indicate that there may be ways of either reducing or indeed reversing the impact of labelling even in the field of mental illness.

An evaluation of the labelling perspective

While the labelling perspective has undoubtedly provided a much needed and salutary alternative point of view to the traditional model of mental illness, it has not received unequivocal empirical support. Many of its tenets are difficult to investigate empirically in the first place, but where this has been achieved there has been a mixture of results which has patently disappointed some adherents to the theory.

The main theoretical criticisms aimed at the labelling perspective have been that it fails to account for the primary deviance which might set the whole process in motion, and that it has not really answered one of the main questions that it itself asks, namely, why do we have such an extravagant mental health care system if there is no such thing as mental illness and who are the main beneficiaries of applying the label of, let us say, depression, to a middle-aged social isolate? Perhaps the labelling perspective has become an over-corrective to the traditional view in so far as it denies the reality of any mental illness. The evidence that we have reviewed, and many people's personal experiences, argue strongly in favour of the existence of something like a disease entity, at least in the case of schizophrenia. To rule out this possibility completely is perhaps unrealistic. Labelling may also understate the likelihood that many attemps at labelling can be successfully deflected. It is not the case that psychiatrists, or their equivalents in other fields of deviance, are all-powerful and can apply their labels indiscriminately to those who are unfortunate enough to come within their purview. It is even more true that many people who may temporarily adopt the label of neurotic, or even psychotic, for themselves are able to escape from its influence sooner or later. It is not inevitable that the role they are assigned comes to overwhelm their total identity in such a way that they can never return to normality.

What we are left with is some considerable support for what I have called the weak version of labelling theory, namely that applying a label of mental illness in some instances does have more or less serious negative consequences for a number of people. In fact most of the empirical evidence can be interpreted as supporting this position, even though it does not clearly support the stronger version.

In the next chapter an alternative hypothesis concerning the social creation of mental illness will be explored.

Chapter 8

The social creation of mental illness

The construct that has been used as the link between social variables and individual psychological distress in the explanations developed earlier in this book is that of stress. On several occasions it has been offered as the most likely way in which social circumstances are translated into individual problems. The way in which people perceive and respond to stress has been discussed particularly in Chapters 1 and 6 and in this final chapter an attempt will be made to draw together some of the diverse themes introduced elsewhere in this book. A hierarchical coping model will be described which takes as its starting point the inevitable stress which all of us will experience in our daily lives. The theory to be presented rests on the assumptions that although everyone encounters stress it will occur at different rates in different social groups, and that not everyone has equal resources available for dealing with it. The distribution of available coping resources will be determined mainly, if not entirely, by the social categories to which people belong. Some people may therefore be at a double disadvantage. They will be at risk of experiencing higher levels of stress because of their social circumstances and yet may be deprived of many of the ways commonly used to combat stress because of these same social circumstances. Consequently these will be identified as groups particularly vulnerable to psychological disorder.

It may be thought that no one would wish to become mentally ill, but this may be too superficial an analysis. It is conceivable that circumstances may well exist in which some people would find mental illness preferable to an alternative state, given the stress under which they are forced to live. A case is not being made that *all* mental illness is consciously contrived as a way of handling stress. Indeed, not all mental illness is produced by stress in any direct or indirect fashion. What is to be suggested is that a large part of the variability in the incidence of mental illness may be contributed to by the differential availability of alternatives to mental illness in the battle against stress. In this case 'psychological disturbance is not considered as a pathological response to unbearable stress but is to be seen as a valuable adaptive reaction that is resorted to when other forms of adaptation are not available or have been tried and been seen to fail'. (Cochrane and Sobol 1980: 167)

Several authors have suggest that psychopathology develops when the coping resources available to an individual are exhausted by the continued presence of stress (Brown and Harris 1978; Lazarus 1966, for example). However, few have suggested that the symptoms of mental illness, its formal diagnosis and even its treatment, may be sometimes regarded as positive attempts to deal with the effects of stress. If we take as a starting point the assumption that most people will try a variety of other methods of dealing with stress before resorting to mental illness because of its personal unpleasantness and social stigma, the issue becomes one of the availability of the alternative responses and how effective they will be for a given person in his or her particular circumstances. Table 14 contains a list of ways of dealing with stress which have been organized in descending order of desirability.

Type of response	Example	Groups most likely to utilize response
1. Intrapsychic defence mechanisms	High self-esteem	Men, those of high social status, the employed, ethnic majority
2. Stress-opposing experiences	Positive affect derived from success, achievements etc.	Men, highly educated, professional and managerial, wealthy
3. Intimate personal relationships	Spouse, mother	The married, middle class
4. Social support (informal helping networks)	Friends, neighbours, relatives	Women, the married, the employed
5. Other forms of deviance	Heavy drinking, drug abuse, violence	Men, lower class
6. Symptom development	Psychophysiological symptoms	Women, unemployed, poor
7. Illness status	Diagnosis of depression	Women, non-working, poor marital relationships
8. Parasuicide	Overdosing	Women, the young, lower class, those in unstable relationships
9. Hospitalization	Admission to hospital	Women, poor, isolated, unmarried, homeless, elderly
10. Detachment from reality	Suicide, vagrancy, alcoholism	Men, unemployed, single

Source: Adapted from Cochrane and Sobol 1980

The order in which the coping responses have been placed obviously reflects a certain value judgement but probably few people would disagree with the general pattern even if specific details could be argued over. The third column of the table lists those groups which are more likely to have recourse to each kind of coping strategy, although this too reflects a probabilistic judgement rather than hard-and-fast rules. Individual variation within social categories will mean that many individuals outside the groups listed in column 3 may also have access to these coping resources. By listing groups here it is intended to imply that a higher proportion of their members will be able to respond in this way than members of alternative social categories.

The first line of defence against stress rests in the person's own *self-esteem*. Many authors have pointed to the very great importance of self-esteem in enabling the person to defend himself against stress. American sociologist Howard Kaplan (1972) in particular has stressed the centrality of self-esteem in explaining why some people resort to a whole range of deviant behaviours, not just mental illness, while others do not. His argument is that one of our central psychological concerns is with the maintenance of positive self attitudes and the avoidance of self-derogation. People who are unable to maintain adequate self-esteem in the face of stressful and personally threatening experiences are expected by Kaplan to display symptoms of severe subjective distress including anxiety, depression and behavioural disorientation.

Kaplan's own research, as well as that of others, has indicated quite clearly that certain groups are much better able to maintain high self-esteem and hence to handle the effects of stress than are other groups. It is, for example, sometimes the case that studies have shown men to have higher levels of self-esteem than women. This is in large measure due to the differential status accorded to men and women in our society. As was discussed in Chapter 3, masculine characteristics are much more highly regarded in general than are those usually considered typical of women. Men are also more likely to be employed in occupations which afford them the possibility of self-esteem enhancement since even those women who are at work are more likely to be in lower status, and therefore less personally rewarding jobs. Other groups which suffer social rejection or stigmatization, such as the unemployed and minority ethnic groups in a prejudiced society, are also likely to have difficulty maintaining a high level of self-esteem.

The second of the coping responses listed is also likely to contribute indirectly to the individual's level of self-esteem. As Phillips (1968) showed quite clearly, the occurrence of events and experiences which provide a *positive input* into the person's psychological world, such as achieving success at work or receiving positive responses from others, is a powerful antidote to the effects of life's negative experiences. Again, this source of positive affect is more likely to be available to men and to those in jobs which provide a career structure and opportunities for concrete achievements and social recognition. The relatively wealthy person (who may also, of course, be in one of the occupations just mentioned) will have the most obvious resource of all available to them – money – with which to ensure that at least a modicum of positive affect enters their lives. They will be able to derive satisfaction from material possessions, interesting and rewarding leisure pursuits, buying desirable environmental assets, and even perhaps from the mere possession of a healthy bank balance.

In the chapter on the psychological aspects of stress the vital importance of the availability of *intimate personal relationships* was discussed in some detail. Perhaps the most important function that this kind of relationship fulfils is the provision of a source of intense satisfaction and positive feelings about the self. It is probably not necessary to cite psychological research evidence concerning the importance of being loved and feeling needed when facing misfortune in other spheres of life. The feelings of personal worth and value that can be gained from close relationships may help people to withstand even the most extreme forms of stress (so long as the relationship itself is not the source of the stress or its existence threatened by the stress). Intimate personal relationships may also function as a refuge and an opportunity for at least relieving some of the stress produced by environmental events merely by providing someone with whom to share disappointments and anxieties. Personal relationships of this degree of intimacy are more likely to be available to the married or to those living in a stable marital-type relationship. It is, of course, by no means the case that all those in this position do have a relationship of a sufficient degree of closeness to provide all the protections possible; marriage can be a major source of psychological distress. Brown in his study in Camberwell found, for example, that the existence of a psychologically satisfying relationship with a husband or boyfriend was much less frequent among working-class women than it was among middle-class women (Brown and Harris 1978). This was particularly true when women had children at home.

To the extent that women are more likely to confide in others about life's problems and their psychological responses to them, they may be considered more able to utilize the resources of an intimate personal relationship if one does exist. On the other hand, men may be considered more likely to derive overall satisfaction from a marital relationship, even if they do not discuss specific problems with their wives, because they are often able to enjoy the benefits of such a relationship, such as home comforts, status, and social support, without enduring the costs that fall upon many women in terms of housework and child care.

Social networks involving less intense emotional relationships are also useful in managing stress. While women are often considered more likely to talk about emotional problems outside the immediate family context, men, because of the cultural definitions of appropriate sex role behaviour, may find it difficult to admit to anxieties, fears and depressions. Being seen to be unable to cope with stressful events may be interpreted as a sign of weakness by men and thus they may not be able to take advantage of the informal helping networks that are available to them for fear of loss of status. This is not to say that all women, or even a majority of women in certain social categories, can derive social support through helping networks. Women with young children at home, particularly if the father is absent, may be almost entirely socially isolated. One of the important consequences of having a job, even although it may be intrinsically not very satisfying, is the enforced social contact it brings. Particularly if one is able to share stressful experiences with others in similar circumstances (such as being the victims of civil disturbance or mass redundancy) social support does seem to help to mitigate the effect of these experiences somewhat. Cobb (1976) found that the availability of social support not only protected people from developing physical and psychological illnesses in the face of severe life stresses but also accelerated recovery from any illnesses they did develop as a consequence of the stress. It is a common occurrence, for example, for someone who has been bereaved to be visited by others who will recount their own similar experiences and help the affected person through the immediate period of grief and depression.

So far the responses that have been considered are all more or less socially acceptable ways of trying to deal with the effects of stress. They are techniques which are not only looked upon in a positive light but are sometimes deliberately inculcated by psychiatrists, psychologists and social workers as coping skills where they believe these to be lacking. The remainder of the responses contained in Table 14 reflect what is often considered *deviant behaviour* of a more or less serious kind. The nature of the deviance entered into at this stage in the process will itself be heavily influenced by social characteristics. Men are much more likely than women to respond to incipient psychological problems with heavy drinking, and with intra-family violence. This is particularly true of lower class men who may be less likely to have available to them sophisticated psychological explanations for their own feelings of malaise than their more educated middle-class counterparts. In some sections of the male working-class subculture heavy drinking is not regarded as particularly deviant and it may be easier for a person in this environment to drift into alcoholism. Again it is worth repeating that it is not the intention to suggest that only men, or indeed only working-class men, can become alcoholic. What is suggested is that social definitions make this a much more likely response for this particular subgroup than for others.

Although it occurs lower in the hierarchy suggested in Table 14 because it usually follows the achievement of illness status, an equivalent female form of deviant behaviour is drug overdosing. This is not usually the result of drug abuse but is rather a deliberate attempt, in many cases, to alter social situations by deliberate self-harm. Although overdoses are taken by people of all ages and both sexes it is a behaviour that is very heavily concentrated among young working-class women. Kreitman *et al.* (1970) have produced evidence to show that within specific subcultures drug overdosing is a recognized form of communication and a way of unilaterally influencing social situations. It is apparently regarded as an appropriate response by young women to intolerable social circumstances and almost as a legitimate means of manipulating personal relationships. This definition apparently does not extend to men in similar circumstances, nor to older, more mature, women.

An example of an effective use of this behaviour was provided by a 16-year-old girl in a northern town. She desperately wanted to leave school and gain some independence from her parents who, she thought, were continuing to treat her as a child. When she became pregnant by an older man she hoped that she would be treated as a mature woman (that becoming pregnant may also be used as an instrumental behaviour in some circumstances is also well recognized). Instead her father browbeat her into having an abortion and going back to school. She became very upset, not so much because of her feelings for her child or even her attachment to the father but because she felt unable to control her own life. One evening she swallowed a modest number of paracetamol tablets and told her mother that she had tried to kill herself. In fact she recovered completely after two days in hospital, was allowed by her parents to leave school and became a trainee hairdresser. In this instance overdosing had a distinct and, from the person's own point of view, desirable effect on her social situation. But this is a high risk strategy. Not only is there a definite, even if small, risk of death or permanent injury from overdosing but the attempt at manipulation can also backfire and make the situation worse.

It is at this stage that the gradual progress of the person towards a fully formed and recognized mental illness may begin. The first stage will be the development of recognizable *psychological and psychosomatic symptoms*. These may be seen either as a result of intolerable stress which cannot be handled properly or, in line with the argument made here, may also be interpreted as genuine attempts at adaptation. The occurrence and persistence of psychological symptoms may indeed serve positive functions for the person affected. In much the same way as the symptoms of physical illness are sometimes effective in changing a situation, or the social definitions associated with that situation, so may psychological symptoms be instrumentally effective. A person struggling with environmental stressors may come to decide that his struggle is having deleterious effects on his health and so give up and, by dint of redefining the situation, decide that he has other priorities. Equally, other people in the situation, who may be the source of the stress or may be in a position to do something about it, may begin to act in a different way if they see that the target person is being adversely affected. Particularly in the case of women, for whom the admission of psychological symptoms is not taken as a form of weakness, perhaps because the manifestation of these symptoms is not all that far removed from the common stereotype of female behaviour (see Chapter 3), this may be one of the few forms of influence open to them within certain relationships. Depending upon the point of view taken, this form of behaviour may be seen as a kind of emotional blackmail or as a positive attempt to deal with an otherwise intractable situation. In either case the development of symptoms is something other than a passive pathological response to an unmanageable stress experience.

Take the example of depression. This is seen by some psychiatrists as a way of using psychological symptoms to persuade others to satisfy the depressed person's abnormal goals. These goals are often to gain the support and subjugation of other people. Bonime (1976), an American psychoanalyst, sees depression as a way of life developed by some people to wring the most out of others by exploiting their generosity and sense of responsibility. This is done by making sure that other people are fully aware of the extent of their depressive symptoms and are affected by them. Perhaps because they are so intensely concerned with their own anguish, people with symptoms of depression are usually unwilling to give anything in return to those whom they are able to manipulate. Arietti and Bemporad (1978: 171) cite the case of a man who had an insatiable need to be told that he was loved and appreciated. When his wife's patience was periodically exhausted by these demands he punished her by becoming depressed and tearful until she responded as he wanted her to. He was quite unaware of the destructive effects his somewhat effective but unconscious manipulations were having on his wife's own mental health.

Any adaptive advantage conveyed by the development of psychological symptoms will be multiplied by having a *formal recognition that illness exists*. In our society illness, certified as such by a doctor, confers a very particular status on the person. This status may be deliberately sought and used by a much larger number of people than is customarily recognized. Cochrane and Sobol (1980: 171) list four ways in which the formal recognition and legitimation of illness may work to the advantage of the patient:

1 by providing an alternative focus of concern which distracts from the original stress;
2 by providing a legitimate reason for not actively coping with, or even addressing, a stressful situation;
3 by temporarily removing pressure being exerted by others which may have arisen as a consequence of, or source of, stress;
4 by legitimating pharmacological relief from the tension aroused by stress.

These consequences of illness diagnosis may seem particularly attractive to certain social groups who lack the resources to manage their lives in other ways. Those falling into this category are again more likely to be women, particularly those with poor marriage relationships, who are perhaps unable to communicate their difficulties directly to their spouse; and those who are not at work and who do not have access to alternative coping mechanisms. The use of a doctor formally to validate what may have become a less than totally effective performance of social roles will not be confined to these groups by any means but must, nevertheless, seem a particularly powerful weapon in an otherwise depleted armoury of instrumentally effective behaviours.

Cooperstock and Lennard (1979) detail how the medically sanctioned use of psychotropic drugs, such as the tranquillizer Valium, can be a very valuable coping resource especially to women who feel powerless to alter intensely stressful and frustrating personal situations. Both because they are more likely to experience prolonged role conflicts, and because conflict is virtually insoluble by any other acceptable means, women are much more likely than men to ask their doctors for help and to receive prescriptions for tranquillizers. Skegg *et al.* (1977), found that 21 per cent of all women compared to less than 10 per cent of men were prescribed psychotropic drugs during a one-year period.

The ultimate consequence of the sick role is, of course, *admission to a hospital*. Although most people would consider a sojourn in a mental hospital as an experience to be avoided at any cost, there are undoubtedly some people who gain considerable benefit from such an episode in their lives. I do not here mean people who receive particularly effective treatment for their condition but rather those who manage to alter their social situation dramatically by a period of hospitalization. This may be effected by temporarily removing the patient from the stressful situation and by altering the way in which others act towards the patient. An extreme case of this might be where a person in trouble with the police was able to alter the decision or response of a court because of his psychiatric status. In less dramatic fashion a whole panoply of helping agencies may swing into action to help psychiatric patients cope with housing difficulties, interpersonal relationships, children, financial difficulties, and petty bureaucratic arrangements. Although it is not being suggested that this is the only reason for their higher rates of inpatient treatment, statistics consistently bear out the fact that women, the poor and isolated, the unemployed, the homeless and the elderly are all much more likely to be referred for inpatient treatment than are other social groups. The argument here is that this reflects the lack of alternative coping resources at least as much as it reflects the excessive stress borne by these particular groups. Particularly among people who have been admitted to hospital in the past, or who have remained in hospital for a prolonged period, a kind of dependency on the institution may occur. This can result in an extreme reluctance to leave the relatively sheltered environment provided by any hospital or a predilection for seeking admission in the face of even the most apparently insignificant frustration encountered outside.

One final stage is included in the hierarchy of coping responses for completeness. This is *detachment from reality* which may *in extremis* be seen as an attempt to deal with a situation rather than as a giving-up response. This time the chosen method of coping is not to manipulate, directly or indirectly, the source of stress but rather for the person to remove himself, physically or psychologically, from the experience of stress. Almost by definition these kinds of responses will be a last resort only, when all other responses have been tried and seen to fail, or the stress experience is so intense as to make any other form of coping appear totally inadequate.

With the exception of level 10 most people will have tried several of these forms of coping with stress in the course of a lifetime. They may be tried sequentially in the course of dealing with a particular incident of stress or, more likely, they may be tried in differing circumstances. Those which prove particularly effective for the individual may be more likely to be tried on subsequent occasions. The girl who took a drug overdose may have learned to try this same tactic in future crises. Conversely those that prove ineffective after several trials are likely to be dropped from the individual's behavioural repertoire.

It bears repeating that this scheme is not offered as a complete explanation for the development of all mental illness, only for that part of it which is capable of being seen as in some way environmentally adaptive. For those people with suitable social characteristics the use of psychological symptoms and mental illness as an adaptive mechanism will probably never be required. For those without these characteristics society may have left them with few options when confronted with stress other than becoming mentally ill.

Society can thus be seen as responsible for promoting mental illness in two respects. First, by putting some of its members in more stress-inducing situations than others and, secondly, by depriving them of the material and psychological resources required for dealing with such stress. It is perhaps little to be wondered at that many people who apparently benefit greatly from a particular course of psychiatric treatment relapse very quickly when they are returned to their original social environment with their coping resources unimproved. People who find themselves in desperate circumstances will resort to desperate measures when all else fails. Unfortunately it is all too often the case that the causes of desperation lie not within individuals but in the social world to which they belong.

Appendix 1
The Langner 22-Item Scale

* For each item the starred response is scored as 1, other responses as 0 (range of scores 0–22)

I would like to ask you some questions about how you have been feeling in yourself lately. I do not want any details, just 'Yes' or 'No' will usually be enough.

1	Do you feel weak all over much of the time?	No Yes*
2	Have you had periods of days, weeks or months when you could not take care of things because you could not get going?	Yes* No
3	In general, would you say that most of the time you are in good spirits, or low spirits?	Good Low*
4	Do you suddenly feel hot all over every so often?	Yes* No
5	Have you ever been bothered by your heart beating hard?	Often* Sometimes Never
6	Would you say your appetite is poor, fair, or good?	Poor* Fair Good
7	Do you have periods of such great restlessness that you cannot sit still very long?	Yes* No
8	Are you the worrying type?	Yes* No

9	Have you ever been bothered by shortness of breath when you were not exercising or working hard?	Often* Sometimes Never
10	Are you ever bothered by nervousness (irritable, fidgety, tense)?	Often* Sometimes Never
11	Have you ever had any fainting spells (lost consciousness)?	Never A few times More than a few times*
12	Do you have any trouble getting to sleep or staying asleep?	Often* Sometimes Never
13	Are you bothered by stomach trouble several times a week?	Yes* No
14	Is your memory all right (good)?	Yes No*
15	Have you ever been bothered by cold sweats?	Often* Sometimes Never
16	Do your hands ever tremble enough to bother you?	Often* Sometimes Never
17	Does there seem to be a fullness in your head or nose much of the time?	Yes* No
18	Do you have personal worries that get you down physically (make you physically ill)?	Yes* No
19	Do you feel somewhat apart even among friends (apart, isolated, alone)?	Yes* No
20	Would you say that nothing ever turns out for you the way you want it to?	Yes* No
21	Are you ever troubled with headaches or pains in the head?	Often* Sometimes Never
22	Do you find that you sometimes cannot help wondering if anything is worthwhile any more?	Yes* No

Appendix 2
The Life Events Inventory

* The weights do not appear in the self administered version. The total score is derived by summing the weights of the events endorsed.

Event	Weight*

Please put a tick by each event which has happened to you during the past year.

Section 1. To be completed by all respondents

—	1. Unemployment (of head of household)	68
—	2. Trouble with superiors at work	40
—	3. New job in same line of work	31
—	4. New job in new line of work	46
—	5. Change in hours or conditions in present job	31
—	6. Promotion or change of responsibilities at work	39
—	7. Retirement	54
—	8. Moving house	42
—	9. Purchasing own house (taking out mortgage)	40
—	10. New neighbours	18
—	11. Quarrel with neighbours	26
—	12. Income increased substantially (25%)	35
—	13. Income decreased substantially (25%)	62
—	14. Getting into debt beyond means of repayment	66

__ 15. Going on holiday   29

__ 16. Conviction for minor violation (e.g.   34
speeding or drunkenness)

__ 17. Jail sentence   75

__ 18. Involvement in fight   38

__ 19. Immediate family member starts   65
drinking heavily

__ 20. Immediate family member attempts   66
suicide

__ 21. Immediate family member sent to prison   61

__ 22. Death of immediate family member   69

__ 23. Death of a close friend   55

__ 24. Immediate family member seriously ill   59

__ 25. Gain of new family member (immediate)   43

__ 26. Problems related to alcohol or drugs   59

__ 27. Serious restriction to social life   49

__ 28. Period of homelessness (hostel or   51
sleeping rough)

__ 29. Serious physical illness or injury   65
requiring hospital treatment

__ 30. Prolonged ill health requiring treatment   48
by own doctor

__ 31. Sudden and serious impairment of vision   59
or hearing

__ 32. Unwanted pregnancy   70

__ 33. Miscarriage   65

__ 34. Abortion   63

__ 35. Sex difficulties   57

Section 2. Ever-married respondents only

__ 36. Marriage   50

__ 37. Pregnancy (or of wife)   49

__ 38. Increase in number of arguments with   55
spouse

__ 39. Increase in number of arguments with   43
other immediate family members (e.g.
children)

__ 40. Trouble with other relatives (e.g.   38
in-laws)

__ 41. Son or daughter left home   44

__ 42. Children in care of others   54

__	43. Trouble or behaviour problems in own children	49
__	44. Death of spouse	86
__	45. Divorce	75
__	46. Marital separation	70
__	47. Extra-marital sexual affair	61
__	48. Breakup of affair	47
__	49. Infidelity of spouse	68
__	50. Marital reconciliation	53
__	51. Wife begins or stops work	34

Section 3. Never-married respondents only

__	52. Break up with steady boy or girl friend	51
__	53. Problems related to sexual relationship	54 ✓
__	54. Increase in number of family arguments (e.g. with parents)	43 ✓
__	55. Breakup of family	77

References

Andrews, G., Tennant, C., Hewson, D. M. and Vaillant, G. E. (1978) Life events stress, social support, coping style, and risk of psychological impairment, *Journal of Nervous and Mental Disease*, **166**, 307–15.

Antunes, G., Gordon, C., Gaitz, C. M. and Scott, J. (1974) Ethnicity, socioeconomic status, and the etiology of psychological distress, *Sociology and Social Research*, **58**, 361–8.

Arietti, S. and Bemporad, J. (1978) *Severe and mild depression: a psychotherapeutic approach*, Tavistock Publications, London.

Bagley, C. (1972) A comparative study of mental illness amongst immigrant groups in Britain, *Revue Ethnies*, **1**, 24–36.

Bagley, C. (1975) Sequels of alienation: West Indian migrants in Britain. Ch. 2, pp. 57–81 in Glaser, K. (ed.), *Case Studies in Human Rights and Fundamental Freedoms*, Vol. II, Nijhoff, The Hague.

Banfield, E. C. (1970) *The unheavenly city: the nature and future of our urban crisis*, Little, Brown & Co., Boston.

Bean, P. (1979) Psychiatrists' assessment of mental illness: a comparison of some aspects of T. Scheff's approach to labelling theory, *British Journal of Psychiatry*, **135**, 122–8.

Becker, H. S. (1963) *Outsiders: studies in the sociology of deviance*, Free Press, Glencoe, Illinois.

Birtchnell, J. (1971) Social class, parental social class, and social mobility in psychiatric patients and general population controls, *Psychological Medicine*, **1**, 209–21.

Bonime, W. (1976) The psychodynamics of neurotic depression, *Journal of the American Academy of Psychoanalysis*, **4**, 301–26.

Booth, A. (1976) *Urban crowding and its consequences*, Praeger, New York.

Booth, A. and Cowell, J. (1976) The effects of crowding upon health, *Journal of Health and Social Behavior*, **17**, 204–20.

Booth, A. and Edwards, J. N. (1976) Crowding and family relations, *American Sociological Review*, **41**, 308–21.

Brenner, M. H. (1973) *Mental illness and the economy*, Harvard University Press, Cambridge, Massachusetts.

Brenner, M. H. (1976) *Estimating the social costs of national economic policy: implications for mental and physical health and criminal aggression*, Publ. No. 78–6660, US Government Printing Office, Washington, DC.

Broverman, K., Broverman, D., Clarkson, F., Rosenkrantz, P. and Vogel, S. (1970) Sex role stereotypes and clinical judgements of mental health, *Journal of Consulting and Clinical Psychology*, **34**, 1–7.

Brown, G. W. and Harris, T. (1978) *Social Origins of Depression: A Study of Psychiatric Disorder in Women*, Tavistock Publications, London.

Brown, G. W., Harris, T. O. and Peto, J. (1973) Life events and psychiatric disorder. Part 2. Nature of a causal link, *Psychological Medicine*, **3**, 159–76.

Calhoun, J. B. (1962) Population density and social pathology, *Scientific American*, **206**, 139–48.

Carmen, E., Russo, N. F. and Miller, J. B (1981) Inequality and women's mental health: an overview, *American Journal of Psychiatry*, **138**, 1319–30.

Catalano, R. and Dooley, D. (1977) Economic predictors of depressed mood and stressful life events, *Journal of Health and Social Behavior*, **18**, 292–307.

Christian, J. J., Flyger, V. and Davis, D. E. (1960) Factors in mass mortality of a herd of sika deer (*Cervus nippon*), *Chesapeake Science*, **1**, 79–95.

Clough, G. C. (1965) Lemmings and population problems, *American Scientist*, **53**, 99–112.

Clout, I. (1962) Psychiatric illness in a new town practice, *Lancet*, 31 May, p. 683.

Cobb, S. (1976) Social support as a moderator of life stress, *Psychosomatic Medicine*, **38**, 300–314.

Cochrane, R. (1977) Mental illness in immigrants to England and Wales: an analysis of mental hospital admissions, 1971, *Social Psychiatry*, **12**, 25–35.

Cochrane, R. (1979a) A comparative study of the adjustment of Irish, Indian and Pakistani immigrants to England, *The Mahesh Desai Memorial Lecture of the British Psychological Society*.

Cochrane, R. (1979b) Psychological and behavioural disturbance in West Indians, Indians and Pakistanis in Britain: a comparison of rates among children and adults, *British Journal of Psychiatry*, **134**, 201–10.

Cochrane, R. (1980a) A comparative evaluation of the Symptom Rating Test and the Langner 22-Item Index for use in epidemiological surveys, *Psychological Medicine*, **10**, 115–24.

Cochrane, R. (1980b) Mental illness in England, in Scotland and in Scots living in England, *Social Psychiatry*, **15**, 9–15.

Cochrane, R. (1981) A survey of psychological morbidity in Pakistani immigrants to England. Paper read at Royal College of Psychiatrists, London.

Cochrane, R. and Robertson, A. (1973) The Life Events Inventory: a measure of the relative severity of psychosocial stressors, *Journal of Psychosomatic Research*, **17**, 135–9.

Cochrane, R. and Robertson, A. (1975) Stress in the lives of parasuicides, *Social Psychiatry*, **10**, 161–71.

Cochrane, R. and Sobol, M. (1980) Life stresses and psychological consequences, Ch. 6. pp. 151–82 in Feldman, P. and Orford, J. (eds), *The Social Psychology of Psychological Problems*, Wiley, Chichester.

Cochrane, R. and Stopes-Roe, M. (1977) Psychological and social adjustment of Asian immigrants to Britain: a community survey, *Social Psychiatry*, **12**, 195–207.

Cochrane, R. and Stopes-Roe, M. (1979) Psychological disturbance in Ireland, in England and in Irish emigrants to

England: a comparative study, *Economic and Social Review*, **10**, 301–20.

Cochrane, R. and Stopes-Roe, M. (1980a) Factors affecting the distribution of psychological symptoms in urban areas of England, *Acta Psychiatrica Scandinavica*, **61**, 445–60.

Cochrane, R. and Stopes-Roe, M. (1980b) The mental health of immigrants, *New Community*, VIII, 1 and 2, 123–8.

Cochrane, R. and Stopes-Roe, M. (1981a) Psychological symptom levels in Indian immigrants to England – a comparison with natives, *Psychological Medicine*, **11**, 319–27.

Cochrane, R. and Stopes-Roe, M. (1981b) Social class and psychological disorder in natives and immigrants to Britain, *International Journal of Social Psychiatry*, **27**, 173–82.

Cochrane, R. and Stopes-Roe, M. (1981c) Women, marriage, employment and mental health, *British Journal of Psychiatry*, **139**, 373–81.

Cockerham, W. C. (1981) *Sociology of Mental Disorder*, Prentice Hall, Englewood Cliffs, New York.

Cohn, R. M. (1978) The effect of employment status change on self-attitudes, *Social Psychology*, **41**, 81–93.

Commission for Racial Equality (1978) *Ethnic minorities in Britain: statistical background*, Commission for Racial Equality, London.

Community Relations Commission (1976) *Aspects of mental health in a multi-cultural society*, Community Relations Commission, London.

Cooperstock, R. and Lennard, H. L. (1979) Some social meanings of tranquillizer use, *Sociology of Health and Illness*, **1**, 331–47.

Coser, L. A. (1956) *The Functions of Conflict*, The Free Press, Glencoe, Illinois.

Day, R. (1981) Life events and schizophrenia: the 'triggering' hypothesis, *Acta Psychiatrica Scandinavica*, **64**, 97–122.

DHSS (1980) *In-patient statistics from the mental health enquiry for England 1977*, HMSO, London.

Doherty, E. G. (1975) Labeling effects in psychiatric hospitalization, *Archives of General Psychiatry*, **32**, 562–72.

Dohrenwend, B. P. and Dohrenwend, B. S. (1969) *Social Status and Psychological Disorder: A Causal Inquiry*, John Wiley, New York.

Dohrenwend, B. P. and Dohrenwend, B. S. (1974) Psychiatric disorders in urban settings, Vol. II, Ch. 29. pp. 424–47 in Arietti, S. and Caplan, G. (eds), *American Handbook of Psychiatry*, Basic Books, New York.

Dohrenwend, B. S. (1973) Social status and life events, *Journal of Personality and Social Psychology*, **28**, 225–36.

Dooley, D. and Catalano, R. (1979) Economic, life and disorder changes: time series analyses, *American Journal of Community Psychology*, **7**, 381–96.

Dunham, H. W. (1965) *Community and Schizophrenia: An Epidemiological Analysis*, Wayne State University Press, Detroit.

Dunham, H. W. (1977) Schizophrenia: the impact of sociocultural factors, *Hospital Practice*, **12**, 61–8.

Factor, R. M. and Waldron, I. (1973) Contemporary population densities and human health, *Nature*, **243**, 381–4.

Fanning, D. M. (1967) Families in flats, *British Medical Journal*, **4**, 382–6.

Faris, R. E. and Dunham, H. W. (1939) *Mental Disorders in Urban Areas*, University of Chicago Press, Chicago.

Finlay-Jones, R. and Eckhardt, B. (1981) Psychiatric disorder among the young employed, *Australian and New Zealand Journal of Psychiatry*, **15**, 265–70.

Fontana, A. F., Marcus, J. L., Noel, B. and Rakusin, J. M. (1972) Prehospitalization coping styles of psychiatric patients: the goal-directedness of life events, *Journal of Nervous and Mental Disease*, **155**, 311–21.

Fox, J. W. (1980) Gove's specific sex-role theory of mental illness: a research note, *Journal of Health and Social Behavior*, **21**, 260–67.

Fraser, R. M. (1971) The cost of commotion: an analysis of the psychiatric sequelae of the 1969 Belfast riots, *British Journal of Psychiatry*, **118**, 257–64.

Freedman, J. L. (1975) *Crowding and Behavior*, W. H. Freeman, San Francisco.

Freedman, J. L. (1979) Reconciling apparent differences between the responses of humans and animals to crowding, *Psychological Review*, **86**, 80–85.

Galle, O. R., Gove, W. R. and McPherson, J. M. (1972) Population density and pathology: what are the relations for man? *Science*, **176**, 23–30.

Garrity, T. F., Marx, M. B. and Somes, G. W. (1977) Langner's 22-Item measure of psychophysiological strain as an intervening variable between life changes and health outcome, *Journal of Psychosomatic Research*, **21**, 195–200.

Gerard, D. L. and Houston, L. G. (1953) Family setting and the social ecology of schizophrenia, *Psychiatric Quarterly*, **27**, 90–101.

Gillis, A. R. (1977) High rise housing and psychological strain, *Journal of Health and Social Behavior*, **18**, 418–31.

Gilloran, J. L. (1968) Social health problems associated with 'high living', *Medical Officer*, **120**, 117–18.

Goldberg, D. P. (1972) *The Detection of Psychiatric Illness by Questionnaire*, Oxford University Press, London.

Goldberg, D. and Huxley, P. (1980) *Mental Illness in the Community*, Tavistock Publications, London.

Goldberg, E. M. and Morrison, S. C. (1963) Schizophrenia and social class, *British Journal of Psychiatry*, **109**, 785–802.

Goldman, N. and Ravid, R. (1980) Community surveys: sex differences in mental illness, Ch. 3, pp. 31–56 in Guttentag, M., Salasin, S. and Belle, D. (eds), *The Mental Health of Women*, Academic Press, New York.

Gordon, E. B. (1965) Mentally ill West Indian immigrants, *British Journal of Psychiatry*, **111**, 877–87.

Gordon, M. M. (1964) *Assimilation in American Life*, Oxford University Press, New York.

Gordon, M. M. (1975) Toward a general theory of racial and ethnic group relations, Ch. 3, pp. 84–110 in Glazer, N. and Moynihan, D. P. (eds), *Ethnicity and Experience*, Harvard University Press, Cambridge, Massachusetts.

Gove, W. R. (1972) The relationship between sex roles, marital status, and mental illness, *Social Forces*, **51**, 34–44.

Gove, W. R. (1973) Sex, marital status and mortality, *American Journal of Sociology*, **79**, 45–67.

Gove, W. R. (1980) *The Labeling of Deviance*, (2nd edn) John Wiley, New York.

Gove, W. R. and Herb, T. R. (1974) Stress and mental illness among the young, *Social Forces*, **53**, 256–65.

Gove, W. R. and Howell, P. (1974) Individual resources and mental hospitalization: a comparison and evaluation of the societal reaction and psychiatric perspectives, *American Sociological Review*, **39**, 86–100.

Gove, W. R., Hughes, M. and Galle, O. R. (1979) Overcrowding in the home: an empirical investigation of its possible pathological consequences, *American Sociological Review*, **44**, 59–80.

Gove, W. R. and Tudor, J. F. (1973) Adult sex roles and mental illness, *American Journal of Sociology*, **78**, 812–35.

Gravelle, H. S. E., Hutchinson, G. and Stern, J. (1981) Unemployment and health: mortality and unemployment: a critique of Brenner's time-series analysis, Lancet, 26 September, 675–9.

Hare, E. H. and Shaw, G. K. (1965) *Mental Health on a New Housing Estate: A comparative Study of Health in Two Districts of Croydon*, Maudsley Monograph No. 12, Oxford University Press, London.

Harkey, J., Miles, D. L. and Rushing, W. A. (1976) The relation between social class and functional status: a new look at the drift hypothesis, *Journal of Health and Social Behavior*, **17**, 194–204.

Hashmi, F. (1968) Community psychiatric problems among Birmingham immigrants, *British Journal of Social Psychiatry*, **2**, 196–201.

Hemsi, L. K. (1967) Psychiatric morbidity of West Indian immigrants, *Social Psychiatry*, **2**, 95–100.

Hess, R. D. (1970) The transmission of cognitive strategies in poor families: the socialization of apathy and underachievement, Ch. 4 pp. 73–92 in Allen, V. L. (ed.), *Psychological factors in poverty*, Markham Press, Chicago.

Hird, J. B. (1967) Vertical living: health aspects, *Royal Society of Health Journal*, **87**, 171–2.

Hitch, P. (1976) Immigrant mental hospital admissions in Bradford 1968–70, personal communication, University of Bradford.

Holahan, C. J. and Moos, R. H. (1981) Social support and psychological distress: a longitudinal analysis, *Journal of Abnormal Psychology*, **90**, 365–70.

Hollingshead, A. B. and Redlich, F. C. (1958) *Social Class and Mental Illness*, John Wiley, New York.

Hooper, D. and Ineichen, B. (1979) Adjustment to moving: a follow-up study of the mental health of young families in new housing, *Social Science and Medicine*, **13**, 163–8.

Hornung, C. A. and McCullough, B. C. (1981) Status relationships in dual-employment marriages: consequences for
psychological well-being, *Journal of Marriage and the
Family*, **43**, 125–41.

Horwitz, A. (1977) The pathways into psychiatric treatment:
some differences between men and women, *Journal of
Health and Social Behavior*, **18**, 169–78.

Ineichen, B. and Hooper, D. (1974) Wives' mental health
and children's behaviour problems in contrasting residential areas, *Social Science and Medicine*, **8**, 369–74.

Jackson, P. R. and Stafford, E. M. (1980) Work involvement and employment status as influences on mental
health: a test of an interactional model, paper presented
at the British Psychological Society Social Psychology
Section Conference, Canterbury.

Jacobs, S. and Myers, J. (1976) Recent life events and acute
schizophrenic psychosis: a controlled study, *Journal of
Nervous and Mental Diseases*, **162**, 75–88.

Jahoda, M. and Rush, H. (1980) Work, employment and
unemployment: an overview of ideas and research results
in the social science literature, Science Policy Research
Unit, Occasional Paper Series No. 12.

Jones, L. and Cochrane, R. (1981) Stereotypes of mental
illness: a test of the labelling hypothesis, *International
Journal of Social Psychiatry*, **27**, 99–107.

Julien, R. M. (1981) *A Primer of Drug Action*, (3rd edn)
W. H. Freeman, San Francisco.

Kallarackal, A. M. and Herbert, M. (1976) The happiness
of Indian immigrant children, *New Society*, Vol. 35, 26
February, 422–4.

Kaplan, H. B. (1972) Toward a general theory of psychosocial deviancy: the case of aggressive behaviour, *Social
Science and Medicine*, **6**, 593–617.

Kapur, R. L., Kapur, M. and Carstairs, G. M. (1974) Indian
psychiatric survey schedule, *Social Psychiatry*, **9**, 61–76.

Kasl, S. V. (1979) Changes in mental health status associ-
ated with job loss and retirement, Ch. 12, pp. 179–200 in
Barrett, J. E. (ed.), *Stress and Mental Disorder*, Raven
Press, New York.

Kasl, S. V., Gore, S. and Cobb, S. (1975) The experience of losing a job: reported changes in health, symptoms, and illness behavior, *Psychosomatic Medicine*, **37**, 106–22.

Kessler, R. C. and McRae Jr., J. A. (1981) Trends in the relationship between sex and psychological distress: 1957–1976, *American Sociological Review*, **46**, 443–52.

Kiev, A. (1964) Psychiatric illness among West Indians in London, *Race*, **5**, 48–54.

Kirk, S. A. (1974) The impact of labeling on rejection of the mentally ill: an experimental study, *Journal of Health and Social Behavior*, **15**, 108–17.

Kirk, S. A. (1975) The psychiatric sick role and rejection, *Journal of Nervous and Mental Diseases*, **161**, 318–25.

Kohn, M. L. (1968) Social class and schizophrenia: a critical review, pp. 155–72 in Rosenthal, D. and Kety, S. (eds), *The Transmission of Schizophrenia*, Pergamon Press, Oxford.

Kohn, M. L. (1972) Class, family and schizophrenia: a reformulation, *Social Forces*, **50**, 295–304.

Kreitman, N., Smith, P. and Tan, E. S. (1970) Attempted suicide as language: an empirical study, *British Journal of Psychiatry*, **116**, 465–73.

Krupinski, J. and Stoller, A. (1965) Incidence of mental disorders in Victoria, Australia, according to country of birth, *Medical Journal of Australia*, **52**, 265–9.

Laing, R. D. (1967) *The Politics of Experience*, Penguin Books, Harmondsworth.

Langner, T. S. (1962) A 22-Item screening score of psychiatric symptoms indicating impairment, *Journal of Health and Human Behaviour*, **111**, 269–76.

Langner, T. S. and Michael, S. T. (1962) *Life Stresses and Mental Health: The Midtown Study*, Free Press, Glencoe, Illinois.

Lazarus, R. S. (1966) *Psychological Stress and the Coping Process*, McGraw-Hill, New York.

Lebedun, M. and Collins, J. J. (1976) Effects of status indicators on psychiatrists' judgements of psychiatric impairment, *Sociology and Social Research*, **60**, 199–210.

Lee, R. P. L. (1976) The causal priority between socio-economic status and psychiatric disorder: a prospective study, *International Journal of Social Psychiatry*, **22**, 1–8.

Lin, N., Simeone, R. S., Ensel, W. M. and Kuo, W. (1979)

Social support, stressful life events and illness: a model and an empirical test, *Journal of Health and Social Behavior*, **20**, 108–19.

Littlewood, R. and Lipsedge, M. (1978) Migration, ethnicity and diagnosis, *Psychiatrica Clinica*, (Basel), **11**, 15–22.

Littlewood, R. and Lipsedge, M. (1981) Acute psychotic reactions in Caribbean born patients, *Psychological Medicine*, **11**, 303–18.

Littlewood, R. and Lipsedge, M. (1982) *Aliens and Alienists: Ethnic Minorities and Psychiatry*, Penguin Books, Harmondsworth, Middlesex.

Lloyd, C. (1980a) Life events and depressive disorder reviewed, I. Events as predisposing factors, *Archives of General Psychiatry*, **37**, 529–35.

Lloyd, C. (1980b) Life events and depressive disorder reviewed, II. Events as precipitating factors, *Archives of General Psychiatry*, **37**, 541–8.

Lowe, C. R. and Garratt, F. N. (1959) Sex pattern of admission to mental hospitals in relation to social circumstances, *British Journal of Preventive and Social Medicine*, **13**, 88–102.

Lueptow, L. B. (1980) Social change and sex-role change in adolescent orientations toward life, work, and achievement: 1964–1975, *Social Psychology Quarterly*, **43**, 48–59.

Lyons, H. A. (1972) Depressive illness and aggression in Belfast, *British Medical Journal*, **1**, 342–5.

McGinty, L. (1974) Rise and fall of the high-rise block, *New Scientist*, **63**, 723–4.

Malzberg, B. (1962) Migration and mental disease among the white population of New York State, 1949–1951, *Human Biology*, **39**, 89–98.

Malzberg, B. (1964) *Internal Migration and Mental Disease in Canada, 1950–1952*, Research Foundation for Mental Hygiene, Albany, New York.

Malzberg, B. (1968) *Migration in Relation to Mental Disease*, Research Foundation for Mental Hygiene, Albany, New York.

Malzberg, B. (1969) Are immigrants psychologically disturbed? Ch. 3.6 pp. 395–421 in Plog, S. C. and Edgerton, R. B. (eds), *Changing Perspectives in Mental Illness*, Holt,

Rinehart and Winston, New York.

Malzberg, B. and Lee, E. S. (1956) *Migration and Mental Disease: A Study of First Admissions to Hospitals for Mental Disease. New York, 1939–41*, Social Science Research Council, New York.

Manis, J. G. and Meltzer, B. N. (1978) *Symbolic Interaction: A Reader in Social Psychology*, Allyn and Bacon, Boston.

Markuch, R. E. and Favero, R. V. (1974) Epidemiologic assessment of stressful life events, depressed mood and psychophysiological symptoms – a preliminary report, Ch. 11 pp. 171–90 in Dohrenwend, B. S. and Dohrenwend, B. P. (eds), *Stressful Life Events: Their Nature and Effects*, John Wiley, New York.

Marsella, A. J. (1979) Depressive experience and disorder across cultures, Ch. 6 pp. 237–89 in Triandis, H. and Draguns, J. (eds), *Handbook of Crosscultural Psychology*: vol. 6, Allyn and Bacon, Boston, Massachusetts.

Marshall, J. R. and Dowdall, G. W. (1982) Employment and mental hospitalization: the case of Buffalo, New York, 1914–1955, unpublished, University of New York at Buffalo.

Marshall, J. R. and Funch, D. P. (1979) Mental illness and the economy: a critique and partial replication, *Journal of Health and Social Behavior*, **20**, 282–9.

Martin, A. E., Kaloyanova, F. and Maziarka, S. (1976) *Housing, the Housing Environment, and Health: An Annotated Bibliography*, World Health Organization, Geneva.

Martin, B. (1977) *Abnormal Psychology: Clinical and Scientific Perspectives*, Holt, Rinehart and Winston, New York.

Martin, F. M., Brotherston, J. H. F. and Chave, S. P. W. (1957) Incidence of neurosis in a new housing estate, *British Journal of Preventive and Social Medicine*, **11**, 196–202.

Millon, T. (1975) Reflections on Rosenhan's 'On being sane in insane places', *Journal of Abnormal Psychology*, **84**, 456–61.

Mitchell, R. (1971) Some implications of high density housing, *American Sociological Review*, **36**, 18–29.

Morgan, P. and Andruskho, E. (1977) The use of diagnosis-specific rates of mental hospitalization to estimate under-utilization by immigrants, *Social Science and Medicine*, **11**, 611–18.

Murphy, H. B. M. (1975) Alcoholism and schizophrenia in the Irish: a review, *Transcultural Psychiatric Research*, **12**, 116–39.

Murphy, H. B. M. (1977) Migration, culture and mental health, *Psychological Medicine*, **7**, 677–84.

Murphy, H. B. M. and Raman, A. C. (1971) The chronicity of schizophrenia in indigenous tropical peoples: results of a twelve year follow-up survey in Mauritius, *British Journal of Psychiatry*, **118**, 489–97.

Murphy, H. B. M., Wittkower, E. D., Fried, J. and Ellenberger, H. (1963) A cross-cultural survey of schizophrenic symptomatology, *International Journal of Social Psychiatry*, **9**, 237–49.

Murphy, J. M. (1976) Psychiatric labeling in cross-cultural perspective, *Science*, **191**, 1019–28.

Myers, J. K. and Bean, L. L. (1968) *A Decade Later: A Follow-up of 'Social Class and Mental Illness'*, John Wiley, New York.

Myers, J. K., Lindenthal, J. L. and Pepper, M. P. (1975) Life events, social integration and psychiatric symptomatology, *Journal of Health and Social Behavior*, **16**, 421–9.

Myerson, A. (1941) Review of 'Mental disorders in urban areas' by R. E. L. Faris and H. W. Dunham, *American Journal of Psychiatry*, **96**, 995–7.

Ødegaard, Ø. (1932) Immigration and insanity: a study of mental disease among the Norwegian-born population in Minnesota, *Acta Psychiatrica et Neurologica Scandinavica: Supplementum* **4**, 1–206.

Pearlin, L. I., Lieberman, M. A., Meaghan, E. G. and Mullan, J. T. (1981) The stress process, *Journal of Health and Social Behavior*, **22**, 337–56.

Phillips, D. L. (1968) Social class and psychological disturbance: the influence of positive and negative experiences, *Social Psychiatry*, **3**, 41–6.

Radloff, L. (1975) Sex differences in depression: the effects of occupation and marital status, *Sex Roles*, **1**, 249–65.

Rahe, R. H., Fløstad, I., Bergan, T., Ringdal, R., Gerhardt, R., Gunderson, E. K. E. and Arthur, R. J. (1974) A model of life changes and illness research, *Archives of General Psychiatry*, **31**, 172–7.

Rees, T. (1982) Immigration policies in the United Kingdom, Ch. 4, pp. 75–96 in Husband, C. (ed.), *'Race' in Britain: Continuity and Change*, Hutchinson, London.

Richman, N. (1974) The effects of housing on pre-school children and their mothers, *Developmental Medicine and Child Neurology*, **16**, 53–8.

Rokeach, M. (1966) *The Open and Closed Mind*, Basic Books, New York.

Robertson, A. and Cochrane, R. (1976) Deviance and cultural change: attempted suicide as a case study, *International Journal of Social Psychiatry*, **22**, 1–6.

Robertson, N. C. (1974) Relationship between marital status and risk of psychiatric referral, *British Journal of Psychiatry*, **124**, 191–202.

Rosenfield, S. (1980) Sex differences in depression: do women always have higher rates? *Journal of Health and Social Behavior*, **21**, 33–42.

Rosenhan, D. L. (1973) On being sane in insane places, *Science*, **179**, 250–58.

Rosenhan, D. L. (1975) The contextual nature of psychiatric diagnosis, *Journal of Abnormal Psychology*, **84**, 462–74.

Rotenberg, M. (1974) Self labelling: a missing link in the societal reaction theory of deviance, *The Sociological Review*, **22**, 335–55.

Rotenberg, M. (1975) Self labelling theory: preliminary findings among mental patients, *British Journal of Criminology*, **15**, 360–76.

Rushing, W. A. (1971) Individual resources, societal reaction, and hospital commitment, *American Journal of Sociology*, **77**, 511–26.

Sampson, H., Messinger, S. and Towne, R. (1964) *Schizophrenic Women: Studies in Marital Crises*, Atherton, New York.

Scheff, T. J. (1964) The societal reaction to deviance: ascriptive elements in the psychiatric screening of mental patients in a midwestern state, *Social Problems*, **11**, 401–13.

Scheff, T. J. (1966) *Being Mentally Ill: A Sociological The-*

ory, Aldine, Chicago.

Schwab, J. J., Bell, R. A., Warheit, G. J. and Schwab, R. B. (1979) *Social Order and Mental Health: The Florida Health Study*, Raven Press, New York.

Seligman, M. E. P. (1975) *Helplessness: On Depression, Development and Death*, W. H. Freeman, San Francisco.

Sergeant, G. (1972) *A Statistical Source-book for Sociologists*, Macmillan, London.

Skegg, D. C. G., Doll, R. and Perry, J. (1977) Use of medicines in General Practice, *British Medical Journal*, **1**, 1561–3.

Sklar, L. S. and Anisman, H. (1981) Stress and cancer, *Psychological Bulletin*, **89**, 369–406.

Slater, E. and Roth, M. (1969) *Clinical Psychiatry*, Baillière, Tindall and Cassell, London.

Smith, D. J. (1976) *The Facts of Racial Disadvantage*, Political and Economic Planning, London.

Spitzer, R. L. (1975) On pseudoscience in science, logic in remission and psychiatric diagnosis: a critique of Rosenhan's 'On being sane in insane places', *Journal of Abnormal Psychology*, **84**, 442–52.

Srole, L. (1972) Urbanization and mental health: a reformulation, *Psychiatric Quarterly*, **46**, 449–61.

Srole, L., Langner, T. S., Michael, S. T. and Opler, M. K. (1961) *Mental Health in the Metropolis*, McGraw-Hill, New York.

Stafford, E., Jackson, P. and Banks, M. (1980) Employment, work involvement and mental health in less qualified young people, Memo 365, MRC Social and Applied Psychology Unit, Department of Psychology, University of Sheffield.

Sterling, P. and Eyer, J. (1981) Biological basis of stress-related mortality, *Social Science and Medicine*, **15E**, 3–42.

Stokes, G. J. (1981) The psychological and social consequences of economically precipitated stress, unpublished Ph. D., University of Birmingham.

Sugiyama, Y. (1964) Group composition, population density, and some sociological observations of Hanuman langurs (*Preslytis entellus*), *Primates*, **5**, 7–38.

Szasz, T. S. (1960) The myth of mental illness, *American Psychologist*, **15**, 113–18.

Szasz, T. S. (1970) *Ideology and Insanity*, Penguin Books, Harmondsworth.

Taylor (Lord) and Chave, S. (1964) *Mental Health and Environment*, Longman, London.

Tewfik, G. L. and Okasha, A. (1965) Psychosis and immigration, *Postgraduate Medical Journal*, **41**, 603–12.

Turner, R. J. and Wagenfeld, M. O. (1967) Occupational mobility and schizophrenia: an assessment of the social causation and social selection hypotheses, *American Sociological Review*, **32**, 104–13.

United States Bureau of Census (1906) *Insane and Feebleminded in Hospitals and Institutions, 1904*, Government Printing Office, Washington, DC.

Vinokur, A. and Selzer, M. L. (1975) Desirable vs undesirable life events: their relationship to stress and mental distress, *Journal of Personality and Social Psychology*, **32**, 329–37.

Waldron, I. (1976) Why do women live longer than men? *Social Science and Medicine*, **10**, 349–62.

Walsh, D. (1962) Cultural influences in psychiatric illnesses in the Irish, *Journal of Irish Medical Association*, **L**, 62–8.

Walsh, D. (1976) Two and two make five – multifactoriogenesis in mental illness in Ireland, *Journal of Irish Medical Association*, **69**, 417–22.

Walsh, D., O'Hare, A., Blake, B., Halfpenny, J. V. and O'Brien, P. F. (1980) The treated prevalence of mental illness in the Republic of Ireland, *Psychological Medicine*, **10**, 465–70.

Warheit, G. J., Holzer, C. E., Bell, R. A. and Arey, S. A. (1976) Sex, marital status, and mental health, *Social Forces*, **55**, 459–70.

Warr, P. (1982) Psychological aspects of employment and unemployment, *Psychological Medicine*, **12**, 7–11.

Warr, P. and Parry, G. (1982) Paid employment and women's psychological well-being, *Psychological Bulletin*, **91**, 498–516.

Warren, C. A. B. (1974) The use of stigmatizing social labels in conventionalizing deviant behavior, *Sociology and Social Research*, **58**, 303–11.

Weiner, B. (1975) 'On being sane in insane places': a process (attributional) analysis and critique, *Journal of Abnormal Psychology*, **84**, 433–441.

Weissman, M. M. and Klerman, G. (1977) Sex differences and the epidemiology of depression, *Archives of General Psychiatry*, **34**, 98–117.

Wenger, D. and Fletcher, C. R. (1969) The effect of legal counsel on admission to a state mental hospital, *Journal of Health and Social Behavior*, **10**, 66–72.

Williams, A. W., Ware Jr., J. E., Donald, C. A. (1981) A model of mental health, life events, and social supports applicable to general populations, *Journal of Health and Social Behavior*, **22**, 324–36.

Wilner, D. M., Glasser, M. N. with the assistance of others (1962) *The Housing Environment and Family Life: A Longitudinal Study of the Effects of Housing on Morbidity and Mental Health*, John Hopkins University Press, Baltimore.

Winsborough, H. H. (1965) Social consequences of high population density, *Law and Contemporary Problems*, **30**, 120–26.

World Health Organization (1979) *Schizophrenia: an international follow-up study*, John Wiley, Chichester.

Yarrow, M., Schwartz, C., Murphy, H. and Deasy, L. (1955) The psychological meaning of mental illness in the family, *Journal of Social Issues*, **11**, 12–24.

Zigler, E. and Phillips, L. (1961) Psychiatric diagnosis and symptomatology, *Journal of Abnormal and Social Psychology*, **63**, 69–75.

Index